e

# 100 bright ideas for
# KITCHENS

**BETTERWAY BOOKS**

Cincinnati, Ohio

First published in North America in 2002 by

Betterway Books,

an imprint of F&W Publications, Inc.,

4700 East Galbraith Road

Cincinnati, OH 45236

1-800-289-0963

ISBN 1 558 70629 1


A CIP catalogue record for this book is available from the British Library


Printed and bound in China


10 9 8 7 6 5 4 3 2 1

# Contents

# Introduction

Your kitchen is one of the most important rooms in your home. A well-designed, stylish kitchen should make you feel happy and relaxed whether you are grabbing a cup of coffee or cooking a three-course dinner. Too often, however, one kitchen ends up looking like a thousand others. This book shows you, first how to create your favourite style in your kitchen and then, how to personlize it with any of one hundred and more tips, ideas and projects.

## Bright ideas
Each chapter in this book is divided into the following four sections.

 **DONE IN A DAY**

Projects requiring some basic DIY skills that you will be able to complete in a day or less.

 **QUICK FIX**

Instant ideas which are simple to do and will take less than a morning.

 **GOOD IDEAS**

A gallery of inspirations for good buys and finishing touches to make a difference quickly.

 **GET THE LOOK**

Whole decorating schemes for you to recreate and adapt to your own style, with tips on how to achieve the look.

## Key to symbols used in this book
Check how long the project will take and how easy it is to do with the at-a-glance guide.

 **HOW LONG** Tells you how long the project will take.

**You will need**
• tape measure
• handsaw
• lengths of 1cm (³⁄₈in) pine board

 **SKILL LEVEL** Tells you how easy or difficult the project is.

easy

medium

difficult

## Plan your kitchen

The first step is to design the layout which suits you best – time spent at this stage is never wasted.

**1** Draw the measurements of your kitchen to scale onto graph paper. Mark on the positions of doors and windows. In many cases, it is possible to move even these to get a better layout, but it is a great deal easier and less expensive to work around what is there, if you can.

**2** Make a wish list of everything you would like in your kitchen, from a cooker and microwave, to a dishwasher, larder, broom cupboard, space for a food processor, kitchen table and so on. Rewrite the list, putting the items in order of importance to you. The chances are you won't be able to fit in everything. Next to each item, write your preferred size or specification – range cooker or built-in, double sink and drainer, under-unit or tall fridge? With some you may have to compromise, while others may be essential to you.

**3** Draw each element to scale on a separate sheet of graph paper, cut them out and label. Take the most important elements – usually the cooker, fridge and sink – and position these first.

**4** Work out how much cupboard space you need. The is the most adaptable part of your plan. Corner cupboards with carousel units make the most of the space, pull-out units mean your larder can be tall and slim, while pan drawers hold far more than ordinary base cupboards. Narrow shelves can be used in spaces where a wall unit won't fit and hanging rails mean you need fewer drawers.

▲  Plan your kitchen units according to your needs. Consider big pan drawers, carousel units to make the most of corner cupboards and pull out racks to access every bit of space.

## Find the right look

When you have your kitchen plan, you can think about the looks you love. This book has five styles to inspire you – the fresh and modern kitchen, the country kitchen, the sleek and chic kitchen, the colourful kitchen and the Shaker kitchen. You will find all the elements needed for when you are choosing a new kitchen plus ideas for bringing that style into your existing kitchen. Just changing the handles and repainting the walls is often all it takes to give your kitchen a stylish new look.

## Find your style

Your kitchen should reflect your tastes and be as personal to you as any other room. Any style can be broken down into ingredients – a 'recipe' to create that look. When you are trying to recreate a certain effect, get used to looking at a room and analyzing the elements which make it up. Look at the materials, styles and colours, whether they blend with each other or contrast for effect. In a kitchen the main elements will be the units – style, material, colour, the walls and the floor. However, it's the finishing touches which give a kitchen its own signature. Handles, window treatments, motifs on tiles and fabrics all make a difference. Equally as important though, are the non-decorative elements – the appliances and the sink, the pans, jars, mugs and utensils you keep on display.

1 **Fresh and modern:** Light, airy, easy to work in, the modern kitchen boasts clean lines but a welcoming feel.

2 **Country kitchen:** Create a homely feel with natural materials, hints of the outdoors and great space and equipment for cooking and baking.

3 **Sleek and chic:** Perfect for city slickers where style is everything. Gleaming chrome and hi-tech materials come together to create a truly twenty-first century look.

4 **Colourful kitchens:** Express yourself in a kitchen that's as individual as you are with bold colours and a lively style. It's made for fun, families and friends.

5 **Shaker style:** A timeless classic, the beauty of the Shaker kitchen is in its sheer, elegant simplicity blended with hand-crafted touches and natural materials.

## Bring in colour

There are no colour rules for kitchens. Just think about the mood you want to create: calm and cool or warm and welcoming. Light, bright colour can make a room feel larger, but think beyond pure white. Sky blue and apple green can be just as effective and are more uplifting. Even in a small kitchen, deep dramatic colour like burnt orange or cobalt blue can look wonderful.

1 **A blast of colour:** Using brightly coloured units combined with a striking colour on the walls will make for a stimulating and lively kitchen.

2 **Using the elements:** The bright fuchsia used on the walls add interest to a relatively small kitchen.

3 **Always accessorize:** Don't forget that colour does not always have to be on the walls and the units – choose brightly coloured chairs, crockery, tableware and flowers to brighten up a plain kitchen.

# Tips and techniques

Here is a quick-reference guide to some of the materials and do-it-yourself (DIY) techniques involved in the projects in this book.

### MDF

MDF (medium-density fibreboard) is a dense sheet material made from compressed wood fibres. Always wear a dust mask when cutting MDF as the very fine dust is harmful if inhaled over time.

### PRIMER

MDF should always be primed before being painted. This step is similar to undercoating wood and stops too much paint being sucked into the MDF as it is painted. You will generally get a better finish when painting wood if you undercoat first, but it is not necessary if you are painting only small areas. If you are painting untreated pine, first seal any knots in the timber with knotting solution. This will prevent the resin from 'bleeding' through the paint and ensure the paint adheres evenly over the wood.

### PAINT

Being water-based, emulsion paint is easy to use, dries quite quickly and is easily cleaned off paintbrushes. It is particularly suited to painting walls. Oil-based paint provides a tougher, moisture-resistant finish. It can be trickier to apply and dries to either a sheen or a gloss finish.

### VARNISH

To protect a decorative finish, an absorbent surface or a water-based paint such as emulsion, use varnish to provide a hardwearing top coat. You will usually need more than one coat of varnish. In most of the projects in this book, an all-purpose, clear, matt varnish is ideal. Sometimes you will need a varnish specifically for wood.

Acrylic varnish generally gives a matt finish, while polyurethane varnish gives a much harder, shinier result.

### TOOLS

An **electric drill** is an indispensable DIY tool. Most drills come with a set of 'bits' of differing sizes and uses. Match the size of the drill bit to the size of the screw you plan to use. Where you are drilling into a wall, use a masonry bit, which is designed to go through hard surfaces. Insert a wallplug in the drilled hole, then drive the screw into the wallplug. When screwing into wood, the drilled hole should be very slightly smaller than the screw so that the screw grips the wood tightly as it is screwed into place. **Wallplugs** are unnecessary for holding screws in wood.

A **panel saw** is ideal for sawing lengths of wood or MDF. To cut smaller pieces into shape, a **tenon saw** is preferable. A **workbench** with a clamp is useful for making sawing easier.

# Fresh and modern

The modern kitchen is designed for today's lifestyle, with clean lines to ensure that no space is wasted and easy-to-maintain surfaces. It's definitely no-frills without being in any way austere. Strong colours and warm wood are welcoming, burnished steel is stylish as well as practical and together they add up to a great place to be, whether you're cooking or chatting.

If you are a modern cook who loves to conjure up the traditional family meal at weekends but who needs good food fast for weekday suppers, this is the perfect style to choose. Your microwave won't look out of place and everything is organized to keep it all close to hand. It's an easy look to achieve, too – with basics in place, all you need are good, stainless steel pans, toaster and kettle, chunky glass bowls and storage jars, plus classic white crockery.

# Mobile breakfast bar

Add castors to a simple, narrow table and you can create a handy place to eat that will fit in even a tiny kitchen.

**1** Lightly sand the surface and sides of the table top and wipe with a damp cloth. Apply a single coat of primer and leave to dry.

**2** Sand lightly to ensure a really smooth finish, then apply two coats of silver spray paint, leaving to dry thoroughly between coats. You can spray paint your castors to match, if they are not steel or chrome. Once the console table is completely dry, apply a coat of matt varnish to protect the surface and leave to dry overnight.

**3** Turn the table upside down, position the castors on the base of each table leg and mark screw hole positions with a pencil. Drill holes for the screws, then screw a castor to each leg.

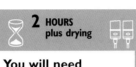

**2 HOURS**
**plus drying**

### You will need
- table
- sandpaper
- cloth
- 3-in-1 primer and undercoat
- paintbrush
- silver metallic spray paint
- matt varnish
- 4 x 50mm (2in) castors with brakes
- pencil
- power drill with 2mm (¹⁄₁₆in) bit
- 16 x 25mm (1in) wood screws
- screwdriver

# Beech-effect kitchen units

Transform plain kitchen unit doors with little more than
rolls of sticky-backed plastic and new handles.

**1** Remove the handles and take the doors off the cupboard unit. Measure the door front and add extra all round to overlap the sticky-backed plastic on to the edges of the door. Mark where your new handles will go and drill the holes.

**2** Cut the plastic to size and lay on a flat surface, wrong side up. Position the door face down, exactly in the centre of the plastic. With the back of the craft knife, i.e. the blunt edge of the blade, mark all round the door.

**3** Lay the door face up on the floor and peel the backing off the top third of the plastic. Position the plastic on the door, using the blade marks as a guide. Smooth down carefully with a soft cloth. Peel off more backing, smooth down and continue until all is applied. Fold the overlap on to the edges, smoothing down very firmly. Cut small V shapes out of each corner of the plastic so that it folds neatly.

**4** Use a pencil to locate the drill holes for the handles, then cut through the plastic into the holes. Screw the new handles in place.

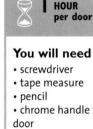

**HOUR**
**per door**

### You will need
- screwdriver
- tape measure
- pencil
- chrome handle for each door
- drill
- wood effect sticky-backed plastic
- craft knife and ruler
- soft cloth

# Colourful tiled splashback

It's easy to tile your own splashback to protect the areas behind the sink and cooker and bring new colour to your kitchen.

**You will need**
- tiles
- felt pen
- timber battens, 50 x 25mm (2 x 1in)
- spirit level
- a few masonry nails
- hammer
- tape measure
- tile adhesive and spreader
- tile spacers
- sponge
- tile cutter
- waterproof grout and applicator
- cloth
- all-purpose sealant

**1** Position one tile centrally under the window, flush with the ledge. Mark where the bottom of the tile falls.

**2** Nail a batten to the wall, its top edge along the marked line, checking with the spirit level that it is horizontal. Measure two tile widths out from the edge of the window, allowing a narrow gap for the grout, and nail a second batten upright along this line, checking with the spirit level that it is vertical.

**3** Spread adhesive over about a four-tile area in the battened-off area. Use the notched side of the spreader to form ridges of adhesive.

**4** Press tiles gently on to the wall until the adhesive squeezes out around the sides. Check the tiles are

flat against the wall. Press spacers into each corner.

**5** Lay tiles along the windowsill so that they cover the top edges of the wall tiles. Wipe off excess adhesive.

**6** Lay all the whole tiles

and leave to dry before removing battens. Cut tiles to fit into any gaps and fix in place.

**7** Grout the tiled area. Remove the excess with a sponge, then leave to dry.

**8** Seal the gap between worktop and tiles with sealant.

# Handy workstation

Turn two coffee tables into an indispensable kitchen trolley that provides extra workspace and storage, too.

**1** Paint both tables with two coats of eggshell paint and leave to dry.

**2** Stand one table on top of the other and draw round the legs. Position right-angle brackets on the table top (one on the inside corners of each leg, i.e. two brackets per leg) and mark where screw holes will go on the top of the lower table and on the legs of the upper table. Drill holes in the table top and in the legs of the upper table.

**3** Screw the brackets to the legs, then place the upper table on the lower table, lining up with the pencil marks, and screw the brackets to the table top.

**4** Screw the rail to the top edge of the table and screw a castor to the bottom of each leg.

**2 HOURS** plus drying

**You will need**
- two identical low tables
- paintbrush
- eggshell paint
- pencil
- 8 right-angle brackets with screws
- drill
- screwdriver
- chrome rail 5cm (2in) shorter than table width
- 4 castors

# Graphic designs

## Black and white pictures

• Frame black and white images to bring simple style to your kitchen. Look for images of fruit or vegetables in cookery books that you could enlarge on a black and white photocopier, or you could even take a

**10 MINUTES**

**You will need**
• image to copy
• craft knife and ruler
• cutting mat
• clip picture frame

picture yourself and use that. Simply crop to fit, frame and hang. Or, prop the frames up in a row along a shelf, as pictured here.

## Leaf-stamped tablecloth

• If the tablecloth is new, wash, dry and iron it first. Lay it out on a flat, firm surface, right side up. Sketch out your design on a piece of paper, then lightly mark out on the tablecloth where your stamped designs will go. Pour a little of each shade of fabric paint into a saucer so that they

**30 MINUTES**

**You will need**
• tablecloth
• paper
• pencil
• fabric paint in two tones of green
• saucer
• small stamp roller
• leaf design stamp
• spare fabric, if required

mix slightly. Apply some paint to the roller, then roll paint on to the stamp. (If you have not used stamps on fabric before, practise on a spare piece of fabric first.) Press the stamp on to the tablecloth, then reapply paint before stamping again. Repeat to cover the tablecloth with the design. Fix according to the manufacturer's instructions.

## Designer tableware

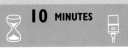

- Practise your design on paper until you are happy with it. Freehand geometric designs look effective and are easy to do. Make sure the crockery is clean and dry before your start. Paint on your design and leave to

**I0 MINUTES**

**You will need**
- plain white crockery
- paper
- pencil
- ceramic paints
- paintbrush

dry. Some ceramic paints are fixed by baking the crockery in the oven – follow the manufacturer's instructions.

## Leaf motif tiles

- Clean tiles thoroughly and wipe with white spirit to remove any residual grease. Spread glue on to the back of the tile motifs and press them on to the tiles. Hold in place for several seconds for a bond to form. Leave to

**I0 MINUTES**

**You will need**
- cloth
- white spirit
- ceramic tile motifs
- strong, all-purpose adhesive

dry thoroughly before cleaning. If you are using plaster motifs, you can paint the front and edges with eggshell paint, allowing it to dry, before applying to the tiles.

# Stylish storage

## Woodstrip memo board

• Use wood glue to stick the pine strips to the MDF back board and secure with panel pins. Apply a wash of emulsion paint, then fix two rows of screw hooks and add a bulldog clip to each hook to hold messages, keys etc. Screw metal rings to the back of the board, attach picture wire and hang on the wall.

⏳ **30 MINUTES** plus drying

### You will need
• wood glue
• 5 x 45cm (18in) lengths of 16mm ($\frac{5}{8}$in) planed pine, 92mm (3$\frac{5}{8}$in) wide
• 45 x 46cm (18 x 18$\frac{1}{2}$in) piece of 6mm ($\frac{1}{4}$in) MDF
• panel pins
• emulsion paint
• screw hooks
• bulldog clips
• screw eyes with metal rings
• picture wire

## Frosted glass jars

• Make sure the jar is clean and dry before you start. Cut a rectangle of the self-adhesive plastic to fit down the front of the jar. Cut a scrap of paper to the same size and write the word you want to etch on to the jar. Tape the paper, with the plastic on top, to the cutting mat and cut out the letters with a craft knife. Peel away the backing and smooth the plastic on to the jar. Apply several coats of glass etch spray all over the jar, leaving it to dry between coats. Remove the plastic to reveal the letters.

⏳ **3 MINUTES** plus drying

### You will need
• plain glass jar
• sheet of clear, self-adhesive plastic
• paper
• craft knife and ruler
• cutting mat
• pencil
• sticky tape
• glass etch spray

## Handy cup hooks

● Mark where you want your cup hooks to go, spacing them out evenly. In soft wood, they will simply screw in, but if your units are melamine, you will need to drill holes to start them off. Place a piece of masking tape over the spot where you are going to drill to prevent the drill bit slipping.

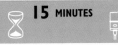

**15 MINUTES**

**You will need**
• cup hooks
• pencil
• low-tack masking tape
• drill

## Useful box shelf

● Hold the shelf up at the height you wish it to be, check it is level and mark the positions of the top and bottom edges with a pencil. Remove the shelf and mark on the wall where the screw holes need to go (this will depend on how your type of box shelf fixes to the wall). To prevent drilling a hole

**45 MINUTES**

**You will need**
• box shelf
• spirit level
• pencil
• 35mm (1⅜in) screws (or those supplied with box shelf)
• drill
• masking tape
• wallplugs
• screwdriver

which is too deep, hold a screw against the drill bit and wrap a strip of masking tape around the bit to mark the length of the screw. Drill holes and insert wallplugs, hold the box shelf up to the wall and screw in place.

# Keeping it simple

## Simplest table runner

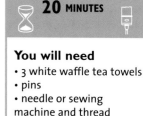

• Lay the tea towels out flat, wrong side up, and pin together the short edges to make one long table runner. Sew the edges together, creating as flat a seam as possible. Press thoroughly and lay on the table.

**20 MINUTES**

### You will need
• 3 white waffle tea towels
• pins
• needle or sewing machine and thread

## Shortcut Roman blind

• On the back of a tea towel sew three rows of three curtain rings, one in the middle and one at each side, ensuring that the rings align across the tea towel.
Cut the batten to the width of the tea towel and fix the top of the towel to the top edge of the batten with upholstery tacks. Screw three eyelets to the bottom edge of the batten, to

**I HOUR**

### You will need
• tea towel
• 9 curtain rings
• needle and thread
• batten
• small saw
• upholstery tacks
• hammer
• 3 eyelets
• drill
• screws
• screwdriver
• strong, thin cord
• cleat

correspond with the three columns of rings. Screw the batten in place above the window. Cut the cord into three lengths, each twice as long as the tea towel. Knot one end of the cord on to one of the lowest curtain rings. Thread it through the rings above and on to the eyelet. Repeat for the other two rows of rings. To raise the blind, pull the cords and wind around the cleat attached at a convenient height on the adjacent wall.

## Bright and white

• It's astonishing what a difference a fresh coat of paint can make, and a makeover in white will make you see your kitchen in a whole new light. Wash all your walls down thoroughly with sugar soap. Go over each wall and fill any chips, holes or gaps with filler. When dry, sand the filler smooth and also sand over any other bumps on the walls. Wash walls with sugar soap again and leave to dry. Paint around the edges of the woodwork, ceiling and corners of the room first with a brush, then fill in the larger areas with a paintpad or roller. Leave to dry and then apply a second coat.

½ DAY plus drying

**You will need**
• sugar soap
• sponge
• wall filler
• sandpaper
• white emulsion
• paintbrush
• paintpad or roller
• paint tray

# Kitchen peg board

• Cut your peg board to the size you want. Hold in place against the wall and, having checked that it is level, mark with a pencil through suitable holes where the fixing screws will go. Remove the board and drill the holes into the board; insert wallplugs. Line up the board against the wall again and screw to the wall. Insert cup hooks in staggered rows across the board and hang up keys, spectacles, scissors, bulldog clips to hold memos and anything else that the peg board will keep usefully out of the way.

**30 MINUTES**

**You will need**
• peg board
• saw
• spirit level
• pencil
• drill
• wallplugs
• cup hooks
• screws
• screwdriver

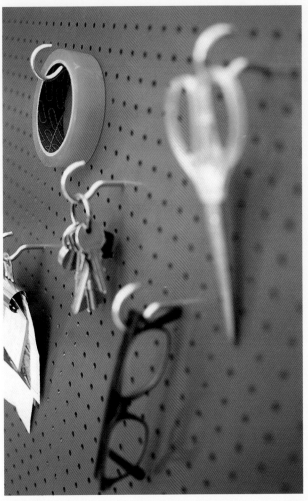

# Metallic magic

A huge range of kitchen equipment now comes in a variety of metal finishes, from high-shine chrome to brushed steel. They fit well in a modern kitchen and don't need a designer name attached to look stylish.

▼ Draining boards are never big enough, so look for a double-decker drainer, which takes up less worksurface space and could even be hung on the wall.

▲ Use a shower rail as a useful place to hang all kinds of small utensils. Simply add butchers hooks.

▲ Conjure up an eating spot from nowhere with a small folding table and chair.

▲ A handy little cupboard like this is perfect for spices or jars and can fit in almost anywhere.

▲ Brushed aluminium looks great: it is easier to keep clean than shiny chrome but still has the reflective qualities that bounce light around the kitchen.

▲ Instead of hiding an unappealing rubbish bin in a cupboard, choose a smart, contemporary aluminium one that will become a feature in its own right.

# Space savers

When planning storage, the trick is to use space to the best possible advantage – so many large cupboards are just full of wasted space. If you are stuck with these, create more usable storage areas by hanging wire racks on the inside of cupboard doors, or by following some of these great ideas.

▼ In a small kitchen, an open shelving unit can make better use of space than conventional cupboards and shows off the wall colour better.

▲ An ironing organizer is somewhere to put away your iron and ironing board. Make it complete with a couple of hooks for your peg bag and hangers for clothes that have been ironed.

▲ Look for a table which folds down to take up almost no space and which comes with a couple of stools that can be tucked underneath.

▲ A wall rack, such as those used in garages, makes a great place for extra storage. Fix to the wall and add butchers hooks and baskets for cutlery, utensils and jars.

▲ Stacking shelves like these are a godsend in cupboards. You can fit in more and get to the plates on the bottom far more easily.

▲ Fill in any little gaps between units with made-to-measure shelves. Even tiny ones will prove useful for jars, recipe books and so on.

# Finishing touches

Sometimes it can be the simplest ideas that bring just the right touch to a look, whether it's a table setting or a storage solution. Contrasts of texture and subtle accents of colour in a natural scheme can be wonderfully effective.

▼ A couple of woven grass bags tucked in a corner come in useful for holding kitchen linens, as well as vegetables like potatoes and onions.

▲ Choose matching jars for all your essentials. They'll look good enough to keep on display, freeing up cupboards and making it easier to find what you need.

▲ Use long, wide blades of grass, washed and dried in the folds of a tea towel, to knot around cutlery for a simple, stylish way to set a table.

▲ A must for addicts of fizzy drinks, a clever dispenser like this stops cans rolling around in the fridge.

▲ Make a place setting look special. Roll up a napkin and tie in place with string or twine. Slip a leaf underneath the string for decoration. Choose something scented, like a geranium, or a sprig of lavender or rosemary.

▲ Give your kitchen a retro feel with frosted glass bottles and drinking glasses, plus a holder for multi-coloured straws.

# Elegant in blue & white

## Create a modern classic with plain white units teamed with warm wood.

The key to the success of this look is to keep everything simple – the duck-egg blue walls and the strong blue of the plain roller blind introduce areas of colour, the pale wood adds warmth without looking rustic and heavy, but it is the predominance of white that gives this kitchen its freshness.

'Laid-on' doors, where the doors are over the front of the cabinet rather than set into a frame, establish the clean, modern lines of the style. To avoid looking clinical, these doors are also edged with wood veneer, which gives an interesting 'frame'. The worktop is made from solid wood, and the flooring keeps the same theme going, although it isn't actually wood at all – it's bamboo, which is a good choice for a modern kitchen as it's more resistant to humidity than wood. The rectangular white tiles forming the splashback are laid brick style – you could get a similar look by painting bare brickwork with white gloss paint.

### What else would work?

- accents of red or apple green
- bare brick walls
- stone worktops and floor

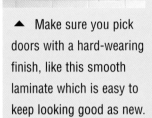

▲ Make sure you pick doors with a hard-wearing finish, like this smooth laminate which is easy to keep looking good as new.

▲ A modern version of the traditional butchers block provides attractive extra storage space and a mobile worksurface.

▲ The modern kitchen doesn't lend itself to busy displays, but coordinated tableware lined up in this rack would fit in well.

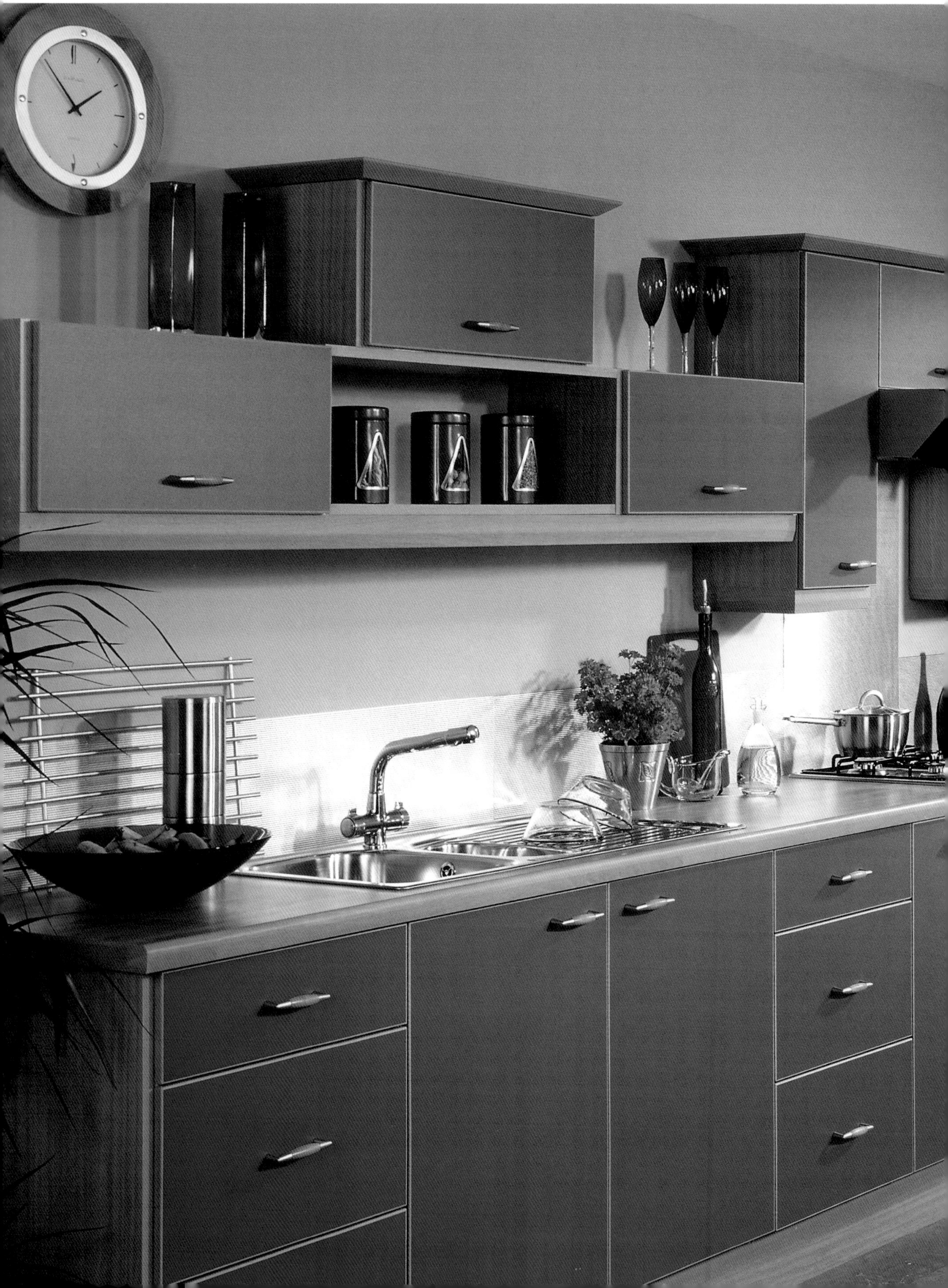

# Smart and streamlined

**An almost monochrome colour scheme is lifted out of the ordinary by an unusual arrangement of wall units.**

Keeping colours very simple is an easy way to create a smart, coordinated look in the kitchen, but you do have to be careful that it doesn't end up looking bland. Here, the imaginatively staggered wall units become a focal point for the room. Low and wide units alternated with display spaces contrast with tall thin units flanking the cooker hob. It's a far less solid look than an unbroken line of wall cupboards.

Everything in this room is in toning shades of grey-blue. The trick is to use different shades of the same colour to create a layered look which gives depth and interest. The doors are the deepest colour, a lighter shade is used on the far wall and a lighter shade again is used on the back wall. It is lifted and set off with beech-effect handles, worktop, plinths and panels. To keep it streamlined, use stainless steel panels as splashbacks behind the worktop and add in blue and chrome accessories.

## What else would work?

- layers of sage green
- beech-effect floor
- brushed-steel handles

▲ Edging the unit doors in beech creates an interesting geometric effect.

▲ Steel and chrome is an essential element of this kitchen where everything appears so simple. The stainless steel sink with a generous drainer becomes a central feature.

▲ A certain amount of storage has been sacrificed by leaving display spaces. Make sure you display things which are used regularly as it will ensure that they do not collect grease and dust.

▲ The doors with their slim frames echo Shaker designs but boast contemporary metal handles.

▲ The huge butler sink is inspired by the country kitchen, but its plain lines are not out of place in this modern setting.

▲ Streamlining traditional style means hi-tech appliances like this stainless steel cooker look at home.

# Mixing old and new

## Create a kitchen with old-fashioned charm and clean, modern lines.

Blending elements of traditional kitchens with modern style kitchens can give you the best of both worlds. Here, different worksurfaces are used around the kitchen – wood for food preparation and granite either side of the cooker for putting down hot dishes.

Space above the cooker has been brought into play by installing a smaller wall cupboard that won't get in the way, with extra slots either side and at the end for recipe books. Simple details like this give the kitchen more interest than a solid run of wall cupboards.

All the colour comes from the rich, yellow units. What gives this kitchen a modern twist is that everything is absolutely plain: the off-white walls do not even have a splashback, the floor is bare boards and there is no curtain or blind at the window. It all adds up to a clean, spacious look that manages to be warm and welcoming at the same time.

### What else would work?

• limestone tile splashback
• limestone flooring
• sage green units
• teak or iroko worktop

# A country kitchen

The country kitchen has to look as if it has been there for years. Key elements are good, solid, wooden cupboard doors, painted or bare, natural stone (or stone-look) floors, range cookers and sinks deep enough to wash up generous casserole dishes. A true country kitchen is completely unfitted, but modern styles let you combine the space and hygiene benefits of a fitted kitchen with open shelving, glass-fronted cabinets and dressers to retain the country look.

This is the perfect style to choose if you feel at home with a bit of clutter, and it is immensely practical, too. Country kitchens don't hide it all away: what is used regularly sits out on the worktop; what is admired and loved is displayed and enjoyed.

# Country-style larder

Turn a cheap wardrobe into ideal kitchen storage by adding shelves and deep wicker baskets. Finish it off by painting the inside of the doors with blackboard paint to make a handy memo board.

**1** Using the spirit level and tape measure, mark out on the inside of the wardrobe where each shelf will go. If the wardrobe is wide, or if the baskets will be heavy, you should also add battening to the inside back of the wardrobe.

⧗ **I DAY**
**plus drying**

**You will need**
- wardrobe
- spirit level
- tape measure
- pencil
- battening
- saw
- drill with wood bit
- wood glue
- screws
- screwdriver
- MDF
- oil-based eggshell paint
- paintbrush
- blackboard paint
- wicker baskets

**2** Measure the depth of the wardrobe from the inside front to the inside back. Cut two pieces of battening to this length for each shelf you are adding. Drill screw holes through battening about every 15cm (6in). Place dabs of wood glue along the length of the first piece of battening and stick the battening against the line inside the wardrobe. Hold for a few seconds then, when dry, screw battening to wardrobe for extra strength. Repeat for each piece of battening.

**3** For the dimensions of each shelf, measure the inside width and depth of the wardrobe. Cut MDF to size, paint both sides and edges of each shelf and, when dry, fit into the wardrobe to rest on the battening.

**4** Paint the outside of the cupboard and give the inside of each door a couple of coats of blackboard paint to create the memo board. Leave to dry before adding baskets.

# Painted kitchen units

Give dated kitchen units a fresh new country look by painting them and adding new handles. Easy surface primer avoids the need to sand awkward bevelled details on the doors.

⧖ **DAY**
plus drying

🖌

**You will need**
- screwdriver
- easy surface primer for wood
- eggshell finish paint
- paintbrushes
- wooden handles or knobs
- wood wax
- soft cloth

**1** Remove all the handles or knobs from the drawers and doors. Coat the surfaces to be painted with easy surface primer, which provides a key for the paint to cling to, so sanding is unnecessary. Allow to dry. Paint the drawer fronts and doors with a couple of coats of eggshell finish paint.

**2** Once the paint is thoroughly dry screw the new handles or knobs into place. Rub wax into the wood with a soft cloth to protect from spills.

# Ribbon detail blind

Punch eyelet holes into a plain white blind and thread through jolly gingham ribbon to create a window dressing with real personality. Vary the ribbon colour or design to suit your own kitchen.

**1** First, sketch out on a piece of paper the final pattern of threaded ribbon you would like on your blind. Plot out your chosen arrangement on the blind using a pencil and ruler.

⧗ **1½ HOURS**

**You will need**
• pencil
• paper
• blind
• ruler
• eyelet kit
• ribbon
• scissors

**2** Use the eyelet kit to punch two rows of eyelet holes, 10cm (4in) apart and at 10cm (4in) intervals.

**3** Cut the ribbon into 40cm (16in) lengths. Snip the ends of the ribbon with a diagonal cut. Thread the lengths alternately through a vertical pair of punched holes and a horizontal pair. Tie each length of ribbon at the front with a neat bow.

# Handy kitchen cupboard

Turn a bookcase into a country-style cupboard by adding a door with chicken wire panels. It makes a great larder, or you could cut out all but the top shelf to create a tweeny cupboard for your brooms and cleaning equipment.

**1** Measure the height of the bookcase, less 5mm (¼in), and cut two lengths of 36 x 63mm (1½ x 2½in) wood for the uprights of the door. Measure the width of the bookcase, less 72mm (3in), and cut one piece of 36 x 63mm (1½ x 2½in) wood for the top width and one piece of 36 x 88mm (1½ x 3½in) wood for the bottom width.

**4 HOURS**
**plus drying**

### You will need
- bookcase
- tape measure
- 36 x 63mm (1½ x 2½in) planed pine
- 36 x 88mm (1½ x 3½in) planed pine
- saw
- carpenter's square
- wood adhesive
- 88mm (3¼in) screws
- paintbrush
- eggshell finish paint
- wooden door knob
- chicken wire
- wire cutters
- staple gun
- 3 door hinges
- magnetic door catch

**2** Glue four pieces of wood in position to form the frame, then screw together. Measure the width inside the frame and cut a piece of 36 x 63mm (1½ x 2½in) wood to make the middle horizontal. Glue and screw together.

**3** Paint the bookcase, knob and frame, and leave to dry.

**4** Measure the top and bottom panels of the door and cut chicken wire to size, leaving 36mm (1½in)

to overlap on the inner sides of the door frame. Keeping the wire taut, staple it to the reverse of the frame.

**5** Fix the door to the bookcase using the three hinges, and finally attach the door catch and knob.

# Multi-purpose workstation

A shelf, a few hooks, a couple of rails and a small, straight-legged kitchen table is transformed into a multi-functional unit. Add castors and you can wheel it to wherever you need it.

**1** Measure from the inside edge of one table leg to the inside edge of the leg to its right. Next measure from the inside edge of the same table leg to the inside edge of the leg to its left. You now have dimensions for the shelf. Cut the MDF to size.

**2** Place the MDF on the floor, stand the table on top, then draw around each leg. Cut out each corner using the saw.

**3** Hammer nails into both inside edges of each leg. Add a couple of drops of wood glue for extra strength and sit the shelf on top.

**4** Varnish the entire table and shelf and leave to dry.

**5** Screw a cup hook near each corner on two sides and on the opposite sides and fix the metal rails. Hang the butcher's hooks from the side rails.

⏳ **3** HOURS

### You will need
- small, straight-legged table
- tape measure
- MDF
- pencil
- saw
- 8 nails
- hammer
- wood glue
- wood varnish
- paintbrush
- 4 cup hooks
- 2 rails
- 4 castors (optional)
- butcher's hooks

# Vegetable motifs

Give tired kitchen doors a new lease of life by painting with sponged-effect squares and vegetable shapes. If you're not sure of your artistic abilities, you could use vegetable stencils instead.

**1** Wash the doors thoroughly and wipe with a cloth rinsed out in white spirit to remove all traces of grease. Sand down the surface to be painted and wipe over again.

**2** Divide the door into equal squares, marking out with the pencil and spirit level. Mask off alternate squares with the masking tape to be sponged.

**3** Pour the first paint colour into a dish and dip in the sponge. Wring out any excess and begin to dab on to the masked-off squares. Build up the colour until you are satisfied with the result.

**4** When dry, peel off the tape and sketch out vegetable shapes on to the door. With a fine paintbrush, paint over the outlines with the orange paint and then start to fill in the shapes, using a dabbing motion to create a stippled effect. Keep the stippling more dense towards the edges of each motif and very light in the centre to create a three-dimensional effect. Leave to dry.

**5** Finish with a coat of clear matt varnish to protect the surface. Leave to dry thoroughly.

**HOUR**
per door
plus drying

## You will need
- cloth
- white spirit
- fine-grade sandpaper
- pencil
- spirit level
- masking tape
- dish
- vinyl matt emulsion in green
- vinyl matt emulsion in orange
- small natural sponge
- paintbrush
- clear matt varnish

# Faux splashback

Use a home-made sponge stamp to fake a tiled
splashback with a bold leaf design.

**1** Paint white emulsion in a band to form a splashback a
little wider than twice the width of a foam square.

**2** Using two or three real leaves as templates, draw a
leaf shape on to each foam square and cut out.

**3** Pour the ochre, brown and terracotta paints in to three
separate saucers. Roller ochre paint on to the first
square and press on to the white splashback area at the
bottom edge. Roller brown paint on to the second
square and press on to the splashback next to the first.
Do the same with the terracotta paint. Repeat until you
have two rows of alternating leaf squares.

⧖ **2 HOURS** 🖌🖌

**You will need**
• emulsion paint in white,
ochre, brown and
terracotta
• paintbrush
• two or three types of leaf
• felt pen
• three squares of thin
foam
• craft knife
• cutting mat
• three saucers
• small paint roller

# Cork notice board

Here's a fun way to use up bottle corks and create a useful noticeboard for the family kitchen. Paint or stain the frame to match your colour scheme.

 **2 HOURS**

### You will need
- 4 lengths of planed pine, 48 x 7cm (19 x 2¾in)
- fine-grade sandpaper
- 55cm (22in) square of hardboard
- wood glue
- 16mm (⅝in) hardboard pins
- hammer
- wood dye or stain
- paintbrush or lint-free cloth for applying stain
- about 170–180 corks
- craft knife
- 2 plates with screws for hanging board
- screwdriver

**1** Smooth off all the cut ends of the pine with sandpaper. Glue the wood to the non-shiny side of the hardboard, to form a frame. Leave to dry, then pin in place from the reverse side.

**2** Stain the wood, following manufacturer's instructions.

**3** Working on a small area at a time, spread a thin layer of wood glue onto the hardboard and arrange the corks. Use a craft knife to cut the corks to fit where necessary. Screw the hanging plates in place on the back of the frame.

# Clever cover-ups

## Chequered floor

● Clean the floor thoroughly and leave to dry. Paint two tiles at a time in your first colour, move on two tiles, and paint the next pair to create a checked pattern. When dry, fill in the rest of the tiles with the second colour.

**2 HOURS** plus drying

**You will need**
• floor paint for vinyl tiles in two colours
• paintbrush

## Wood-grained doors

● Wash down units thoroughly, sand lightly to provide a key and wipe over with white spirit. Paint your base colour in vinyl matt paint. When dry, paint over a coat of woodwash. Working quickly, use the wood-graining tool to create a wood-grain effect. Hold the tool at the top of the door and drag down to the bottom with a light but firm motion, rocking the tool back and forth slowly to create the grain effect.

**30 MINUTES** per door

**You will need**
• sandpaper
• white spirit
• cloth
• vinyl matt paint
• paintbrush
• woodwash
• wood-graining tool

## Pretty covered shelves

• Lay the paper on the shelf. Take closed scissors and run the point around all the edges of the shelf to mark out the exact size of the shelf. Remove the paper and cut out to fit inside the shelves. Spread glue on the

**30 MINUTES**

**You will need**
• wallpaper or wrapping paper with a small pattern
• scissors
• glue
• clear matt varnish

back of the paper, then smooth into place. When dry, apply a coat of varnish for protection.

## Oilcloth table cover

• Place the oilcloth face down on the floor. Turn the table upside down and place in the centre of the oilcloth. Fold the cloth over the edges and staple to the underside of the table (get a friend to help you stretch

 **15 MINUTES**

**You will need**
• table
• oilcloth, 7–8cm (3in) longer and wider than your table
• staple gun

the cloth really tight). Take care with the corners to ensure a neat finish.

# The natural touch

## Fruit preserve jars

● Photocopy the fruit images on to tracing paper and cut out to form label-size squares. Stick the labels to the jars or bottles with spray adhesive. Cover the labels with a layer of clear self-adhesive film so that they can be wiped clean.

 **IO** MINUTES

**You will need**
- woodcut images of fruit
- tracing paper
- scissors
- jars or bottles with airtight seals
- spray adhesive
- clear self-adhesive film

## Rustic windowsill pots

● Cover some containers in fabric and others in paper. Cut the fabric and tear the paper to size. Wrap around the container several times, allowing extra at the top of the pot to be folded over or arranged to hide the top edge of the pot. Bind with string or copper wire and fray the top edge of the fabric.

**I5** MINUTES

**You will need**
- cans or jars
- plain, firm fabric, such as hessian or calico
- thick brown paper
- scissors
- string or copper wire

## Framed fruit

• Cut 3mm (⅛in) thick slices of apples and pears from the centre of the fruit. Sandwich the slices in kitchen paper, then between two pieces of plywood. Put in a microwave, place a non-metallic weight on top and heat for three minutes

**I HOUR plus drying**

**You will need**
- apples and pears
- kitchen paper
- plywood
- microwave oven
- non-metallic weight
- handmade paper
- picture frame

on a medium setting. Take out and leave to cool. Change the kitchen towel and repeat, giving 20 second bursts of medium heat and leaving to cool in between. Change the kitchen towel as needed. When almost dried out, put slices on kitchen paper on a warm radiator or sunny windowsill to dry out completely. Mount on handmade paper and frame.

## Leaf-patterned tiles

• A fun and easy way to jazz up plain tiles. Clean tiles thoroughly and wipe over with a cloth rinsed out with white spirit to remove traces of grease. Pour paint into a saucer and, using the roller, apply paint evenly to the stamp. Position the stamp on the tile, press and hold. Take care as the surface of the stamp can be slippery. Leave to dry.

**40 MINUTES**

**You will need**
- cloth
- white spirit
- ceramic paint
- saucer
- small paint roller
- leaf stamp

# Rural medley

## Slate jotting board

● Many builder's merchants stock slate roof tiles, but if you are using an old tile, clean it thoroughly with warm soapy water and leave to dry. Stick two short pieces of masking tape on to the front of the tile where you want to drill the holes for the twine. Drill holes through the slate, remove tape, then thread twine through the holes, knot at the front and hang up.

⏳ **15** MINUTES

**You will need**
- roof slate
- masking tape
- drill
- thick twine

## Cinnamon stick picture frame

● Cut the cinnamon sticks to size using sharp pruning shears – the sticks can be wider than the frame. Lay the frame face on a firm, flat surface and cover the top edge generously with glue. Lay the sticks on to the frame, pushing them tightly together, across the full width of the frame. Repeat along the bottom edge, then fit more sticks into the gaps along the sides.

⏳ **30** MINUTES

**You will need**
- cinnamon sticks
- small, very sharp pruning shears
- flat picture frame
- strong glue

# Crackle-glazed doors

● Remove doors, sand down thoroughly and wipe with white spirit to remove fine dust and any residual grease. Paint with two coats of your chosen base colour. When dry, apply the crackle glaze with a paintbrush and leave according to the manufacturer's instructions

**1½ HOURS**
**per door**

**You will need**
• screwdriver
• sandpaper
• white spirit
• 2 coordinating emulsion colours
• crackle glaze kit
• paintbrush

– usually around half an hour. Paint on your chosen top coat in even brush strokes and leave. As it dries, the crackling will occur – do not brush after the crackling begins.

# Freestanding drawer unit

● Remove existing handles and prepare the chest for painting by sanding off all the old paint and cleaning with white spirit. Paint the chest all over with two coats of emulsion and leave to dry. Use fine-grade sandpaper to rub back paint on the edges and corners of the chest to give it a distressed look.

**2 HOURS**
**plus drying**

**You will need**
• screwdriver
• sandpaper in medium and fine grades
• white spirit
• cloth
• off-white emulsion paint
• paintbrush
• wicker baskets
• brass oyster shell handles

Remove the front of the top drawer or, if your chest cannot be taken apart like this, remove the drawer altogether. Put baskets in the top drawer and fix the oyster shell handles on to the lower drawers.

# Warm wood and wicker

Bring the country into your kitchen with natural materials. Wood always looks at home, whether waxed, painted or simply left bare and woven wicker offers rustic texture and homely warmth.

▼  No room for a draining board? A pine dish drainer can be folded away when it's not in use.

▲  Wood always looks good in the country kitchen, especially for traditional furniture pieces like this farmhouse plate rack.

▲  A butler tray has many uses; choose a plain pine one and paint it with white oil-based paint.

▲ Bring mouthwateringly warm fresh bread to the table in a deep tray lined with a napkin.

▲ Free up cupboard space with a traditional wall-hung cup holder. Choose one with a shelf above for jugs.

▲ Pile fruit and vegetables into wicker baskets for a real country look.

# Country charm

Despite a constant influx of new gadgets and designs on the market, traditional pieces have a timeless appeal and are easy to live with. A characterful item will instantly contribute atmosphere to your kitchen setting.

▲ Choose old-fashioned balancing scales with shiny brass weights. Not only do they look good but they are among the most accurate and simplest of kitchen scales.

▼ Give plain jars a new twist by wrapping thick lengths of raffia around the middle and gluing the ends in place.

▲ Hand-painted china makes meal times more colourful and is perfect for displaying on dressers.

▲ Use chunky glazed ceramic tiles as rustic coasters for hot and cold drinks (stick felt underneath to avoid the rough back scratching surfaces). Group tiles together as a mat for hot dishes.

▲ A traditional stove-top kettle will boil water for your morning brew as quickly as most modern electric ones.

▲ Make baking fun with bowls, dishes and utensil pots with a farmhouse theme.

A country kitchen

# Farmhouse fresh

## Mix buttercream and terracotta for a warm, sunny feel.

A subtle way to give your kitchen country style is to avoid matching unit doors. Here there's a mix of panelled doors, tongue and groove with quirky drilled holes inspired by the original kitchen door, open shelving and wall cupboards where the central panel is replaced by chicken wire. The door handles continue the mixing of styles.

Where there is no room a for genuine range cooker, choose one of the range-style standard-width cookers with brass trim. Try to fit in a dresser, even if it means sacrificing one wall of standard units. Not only does it fit the look better but a dresser is a very useful piece in any kitchen for displaying anything from pretty china to nostalgic mementoes.

Keep the colours simple. The white tiled worktop is carried up on to the splashback and the lovely terracotta floor tones subtly with the cream and the wood, while the deep green-blue Windsor chair looks all the more at home for not matching the units.

### What else would work?

- inset tiles with raised animal or vegetable motifs
- big range cooker
- units in dusty blue
- all-wood worktops

▲ Country kitchens are no place for bright shiny metals, so choose pewter or unpolished brass for details such as handles. Oyster-shell handles, like the kind found on old-fashioned filing cabinets, add the right touch.

▲ Terracotta tiles make a beautiful country-style floor, but make sure they are well sealed, as terracotta is porous and will absorb greasy spills.

▲ Fill shelves with jars of preserves, recipe books and farmhouse kitchenalia.

# Twenty-first century Victorian

## Rustic pine offset by bold blue creates a a striking effect.

Contemporary touches make this country kitchen so much more interesting. The knotted pine doors with their aged patina and arch-topped panels give the kitchen a nice period feel. Rather than teaming them with a bland colour, however, the walls have been painted in a rich, vibrant blue that really brings the room to life and balances the orange tones of the pine. The worktop uses a mix of surfaces – wood is ideal for a chopping surface, and the granite-look laminate tones with the hard-wearing slate floor. A slatted rack on the wall holds attractive tins and jars of goodies. Pick the best-looking ones and keep the rest in the larder. A collection of jugs sits on the glass shelves while pans too big to fit in the cupboards find a home at the back of the worktop. Meanwhile the traditional back door has been replaced with french doors that fill the room with light.

### What else would work?

- fresh apple green walls
- real granite or marble worktops
- a butcher's block
- pots, pans and jugs in rich red

▲ Cabinets with glass doors give you the chance to show off attractive china and help avoid the kitchen looking too fitted.

▲ That great Victorian standard, the butler sink, is as practical today as it was a century ago.

▲ Flowers and, especially, herbs bring the garden into the kitchen and help recall the days when much of what came into the kitchen was home-grown.

▲ The delicate stencilled designs on the cupboard doors add interest without fussiness. They also introduce a pleasing element of folk art.

▲ Victorian and Edwardian tiles were often highly decorative and these make a charming feature above the hob.

▲ Country style is emphatically not about pattern matching and careful coordination.

# Country cottage

**Traditional florals, charmingly mismatched china and lots of natural wood make this welcoming look.**

Fresh spring green teamed with white walls and wood provides a simple canvas ready to dress up with pretty country details.

Wood worktops are first choice for a country kitchen. Choose laminate for practicality, but if you go for real wood, make sure it's a naturally moisture-resistant wood like teak or iroko. Keep it well oiled and it will last for years. The deep sink with swan-necked tap is a lovely period detail but one with a practical purpose – its great for washing up huge pots and grill trays. The swathe of floral fabric at the window is an easy way to disguise the fact that the window is modern.

Little details make the difference in a kitchen like this, like the old-fashioned drying rack, useful where there is little space, and the topiary tree on the windowsill that picks up the stencilled doors.

**What else would work?**

• pots of herbs on the windowsill
• scrubbed pine table
• rich coral splashback tiles
• ladderback chairs

# Sleek and chic

This style is the most sophisticated look of all for kitchens. Inspired by professional restaurant kitchens, the key elements are steel and chrome appliances balanced with natural materials like glass, granite, wood and stone, with clean, sleek lines for everything from units to handles. There is an emphasis on imaginative use of materials like metal for splashbacks and glass for worktops and on making a feature of functional objects such as cooker hoods.

This is a style that is particularly suited to modern homes, particularly loft apartments and open-plan houses, and it's a natural partner for hi-tech gadgets, designer accessories and the latest appliances. Choose this look if you enjoy efficiency, hate clutter and are prepared to put in the work to keep metal gleaming, wood oiled and surfaces clear.

# Stepped shelves

These made-to-measure shelves add more interest to a wall than a regular block of shelves but still provide plenty of storage space.

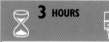
**3 HOURS**

**You will need**
- 5mm (¼in) MDF, 13cm (5in) wide
- saw
- PVA glue
- panel pins
- hammer
- primer
- oil-based paint
- wall brackets

**1** Cut the MDF into shelf lengths, each decreasing by 13cm or 5in: 2 x 76cm (30in), 1 x 63cm (25in), 1 x 50cm (20in) and 1 x 37cm (15in). Also cut 4 x 13cm (5in) lengths and 1 x 55cm (21in) length for the uprights.

**2** Glue and pin one 13cm (5in) length at right angles to first one and then the other 76cm (30in) length, to make three sides of a box, with the longer pieces covering the cut ends of the short length.

**3** Attach the free ends of the 76cm (30in) lengths to the 55cm (21in) piece, which will form the long side panel. Ensure that the bottom of the lowest shelf is neatly aligned with the edge of the side panel and that the second 76cm (30in) shelf is exactly parallel before gluing and pinning.

**4** Lay the 63cm (25in) shelf on top of the second shelf to get the position for the outer edge of the next 13cm (5in) upright. Glue and pin the upright in position, hammering from the under side of the second shelf. Fix the 63cm (25in) shelf in place. Repeat with the final two shelves.

**5** Prime shelves all over, leave to dry, then paint. Fix to the wall with brackets.

# Contemporary doors

Clever use of laminate and stylish handles give ordinary doors the designer look.

**1** Remove the handles and cupboard doors and clean.

**2** Measure the door front and mark the measurements on the back of the laminate. Cut out the sheets of laminate with a craft knife resting on a cutting mat.

**3** Peel off the backing and stick the cut-out sheets of laminate onto the doors.

**4** Position handles and mark where screw holes will go. Drill holes through the doors and attach handles.

**1 HOUR per door**

### You will need
- tape measure
- pencil
- self-adhesive laminate
- craft knife
- steel rule
- cutting mat
- handles
- drill

# Quick kitchen revamp

Paint your doors, attach new handles and add silver mosaic tiles to a plain splashback.

**1** Sand down the doors and prime. Apply the white satin paint with a roller, leave to dry, then apply the second coat.

**2** Position the handles, mark the screwholes, drill the holes and fix on the new handles.

**3** Clean the tiles thoroughly, then snip silver mosaic tiles into separate pieces. Apply ceramic adhesive to the back of a tile and press into the centre of a plain white splashback tile. Repeat for other tiles.

⏳ **I DAY plus drying**

### You will need
- fine grade sandpaper
- primer
- paintbrush
- white satin-finish paint
- small roller
- handles
- pencil
- drill
- screwdriver
- silver mosaic tiles
- sharp scissors
- ceramic adhesive

# Display boxes

Everyday items can be brought together in an imaginative display with this simple-to-make box construction.

**1** Use one of the wooden boxes to work out the size of your plywood back board. Cut plywood to four times the width of the box and one and a half times its length.

**2 HOURS**

### You will need
- 3 wooden boxes with clear glass or plastic sliding lids
- plywood
- tape measure
- pencil
- saw
- drill with 1cm (³⁄₈in) bit
- strong wood glue
- butcher's hooks
- clear matt varnish

**2** Measure 4cm (1½in) from the bottom edge of the plywood back board and mark out the position of five holes for hanging butcher's hooks. From the front of the plywood, drill out 1cm (³⁄₈in) diameter holes.

**3** Position the wooden boxes close to the top of the back board and attach with strong wood glue. Leave to dry.

**4** Fill each box with different pastas or dried peppers. Attach butcher's hooks to the holes and use to hang kitchen utensils.

**5** Screw to wall.

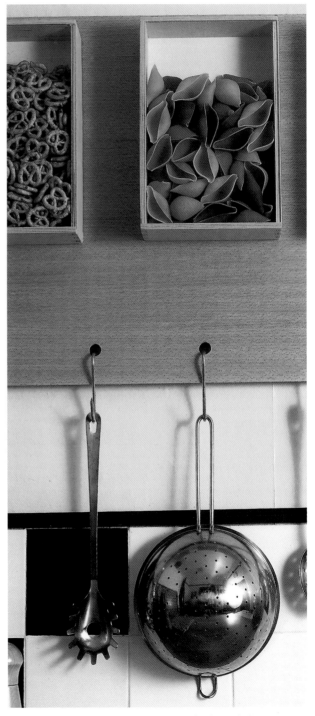

# Designer detailing

## Glass-fronted display boxes

● Remove the glass from the boxes. Work out the positioning of the box frames on the wall so that they stack on top of one another up the wall. Apply extra strong glue to the wall and to the back of the frame

**20 MINUTES**

**You will need**
• box frames with slide-in glass fronts
• extra strong glue
• spirit level

and hold in place for a few minutes until the glue begins to set. Attach all the frames to the wall, checking that they are level. When fixed to the wall, fill with little bottles, spice jars, decorative packets and so on. Slide the glass fronts back in place.

## Glass etching

● Trace the image of a feather on to tracing paper. Rub over the back of the tracing paper with a soft pencil, place face up on the stencil card and then trace over it again with a sharp pencil to transfer the image on to the card. Carefully cut out the design to leave a feather shape in

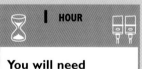

**I HOUR**

**You will need**
• image of a feather
• sharp and soft pencils
• tracing paper
• stencil card
• craft knife
• cutting mat
• glass plate
• masking tape
• newspaper
• glass frosting spray

the card. Stick the stencil on to a glass plate with masking tape and cover the rest of the plate with newspaper to protect it. Spray the image with glass frosting spray and leave to dry for a few minutes before removing the stencil.

## Instant block shelf

• Measure the front and sides of your shelf. Cut plywood to length, 6cm (2½in) wide. Glue and tack in place along the shelf edges. Paint the plywood and shelf and leave to dry.

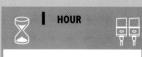

**I HOUR**

**You will need**
• tape measure
• pencil
• plywood
• saw
• strong wood glue
• tacks
• hammer
• oil-based paint
• paintbrush

## Glass splashback

• Hold the piece of glass in position and mark where the screw holes will be. Set the glass aside and drill the holes in the wall, insert wallplugs, then hold the splashback in position and screw firmly into place.

**I HOUR**

**You will need**
• reinforced glass, cut to size by a glazier, with holes drilled in each corner
• pencil
• drill
• wallplugs
• dome-headed screws
• screwdriver

# A subtle gleam

## Wallpaper effects

• Choose wipeable vinyl wallpaper with a metallic sheen and aim to paper walls in alternate designs – or, use the strongest design on one feature wall. Start in the corner where the two wallpapers will meet and hang the frist length, overlaping the edge slightly into the corner. Do not trim at this stage. Hang lengths of the coordinating paper on the other side of the corner, overlapping the edge slightly onto the first length of paper. Take the stanley knife and run a very sharp blade down the corner, cutting through both thicknesses of paper. Peel back the paper slightly, remove the excess and smooth back down into the corner. Continue to paper the room and finish with a border.

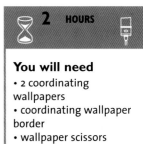

⏳ **2** HOURS

**You will need**
• 2 coordinating wallpapers
• coordinating wallpaper border
• wallpaper scissors
• stanley knife
• wallpaper paste
• pasting brush
• sponge

## Metallic hanging grid

• Measure the side of your cupboard and cut the trellis to size, smoothing off any rough edges with sandpaper. Spray the trellis all over with silver metallic paint, making sure you cover all the inside edges. When it is dry, pin in place, attach cup hooks and hang up utensils.

⏳ **45** MINUTES

**You will need**
• garden trellis
• tape measure
• pencil
• saw
• sandpaper
• silver metallic spray paint
• panel pins
• hammer
• cup hooks

# Improvise a vegetable hanging basket

• Cut three lengths of chain for each basket, making sure the chain will be long enough so that when the baskets are hanging up they will be spaced out sufficiently to get fruit and vegetables in and out. Attach an S-shaped hook to both ends of each chain and attach hooks to the rims of the baskets. For the top basket, bring all three chains together and hang from a strong screw hook attached to the ceiling or under a shelf.

# Gilded pots

• Spread out newspaper to protect your surfaces. Dab a soft cloth into a pot of gilding cream or wax and rub into the outside of a terracotta pot, using a gentle circular motion. Build up the layers of cream or wax as needed to get a smooth, even finish. Leave to dry.

# Contemporary table style

Laying a table for dinner is a good opportunity to try out different design schemes to suit a modern setting. Urban industrial-style, minimalist Japanese and stark monochrome are all promising starting points for stylish food settings.

▲ Pure white tableware with only the simplest of embossed designs has a classic look that works well in a modern setting, and it mixes beautifully with chrome.

▼ For unusual impromptu candle holders, remove the labels from tin cans, wash and dry them, then fill with salt or sand and insert several taper candles.

▲ The oriental look and sleek, chic kitchens are perfect partners; both depend on a minimalist, pared-down style.

▲ Give food a presentational twist by serving it on unusually shaped plates, like these rectangular ones. Look, too for square or oval plates and platters.

▲ Make a quick place setting by cutting a slit in the top of a cork. Write your guest's name on a business cards and wedge it into the cork.

▲ Get exactly the look you want by making your own table runner. This silvery blue fabric has a subtle geometric design woven into it that marries perfectly with the round heads of the globe thistles.

**Sleek and chic**

▲ A couple of stylish fold-up stools tucked away against the wall will always come in handy when you have a crowd around.

# Streamlined storage

Storage is particularly important in a very modern or minimalist kitchen, because clutter is the total antithesis of the style. Think laterally and look for unusual, creative solutions.

▼ Pots and pans can take up a lot of space and are not always accessible when they are hidden away in a cupboard. Update the idea of the old-fashioned pan stacker with a stylish chrome version to hold all your most-used pans.

▲ This sideboard could replace a couple of base units and will provide plenty of accessible storage space, as well as a useful worksurface.

▲　An open shelving rack is a highly adaptable piece of furniture for the kitchen, especially where space is tight and you want to avoid making the room look too closed in with lots of units.

▲　Free up worktop space by mounting your bread bin on the wall. Simply drill a couple of holes in the back and screw to the wall.

▲　You might associate egg baskets with the country look but a chrome one fits well with the industrial look alongside scrubbed-out cans used as cutlery holders.

# Modern materials

This look is all about appreciating materials for their own worth, with no disguising paint or cover-up fabrics. Galvanized and stainless steel won't warp, stain or chip, so will stand up to the rigours of the contemporary kitchen.

▲　Big stainless steel appliances – fridge, cooker, dishwashers, washing machines – all look great in an ultra-modern setting.

▼　It may be expensive, but granite is one of the most stylish and hard-working surfaces you can choose for a worktop. Complement it by choosing well-designed kitchen accessories, like this steel-handled knife set and a chopping board with integral drainer.

▲　Have a few decorative cans and designer gadgets out on display to give your kitchen that hi-tech look.

▲　Look for steel mugs and cafetières to complete the modern look.

▲　Even your utensils can add to the look with contemporary styling in classic stainless steel.

▲　Galvanized steel floor tiles are a little noisy underfoot, but they are incredibly hard-wearing and very practical in a kitchen.

# Loft living

## Think New York loft apartment to get the designer look of this slick kitchen.

Everything about this kitchen says contemporary. Smooth fitted units are faced with birch ply and the brushed chrome rail-style handles run the full width or length of cupboard doors to enhance the linear effect. Brushed chrome has also been used for the plinth at the bottom of the units and the narrow, granite-topped splashback. It's a natural choice, too, for the built-in microwave which sits in a specially designed unit. Rather than floor cupboards, all the units boast deep pull-out drawers, which means no reaching into the back of cupboards for long-lost pans – everything is ultra accessible.

The bare brick walls and pale stone floors give this kitchen the atmosphere of a genuine loft apartment and make it feel spacious, too. If you have the space, go for a range-style cooker. This one is a real space-age version of the traditional stove: extra-wide oven and big burners with hi-tech styling.

### What else would work?

- white gloss units
- polished granite floor
- steel splashback
- chunky glass worktop

▲ Leather chairs and a glass table are an unusual choice for a kitchen but work well in this setting. The chrome chair frames echo the chrome elsewhere in the room and black leather makes a strong statement.

▲ Keep the look streamlined with steel and chrome accessories to match your appliances.

▲ The brushed chrome chimney fitted with a sweep of curved glass makes a dramatic feature of the cooker hood.

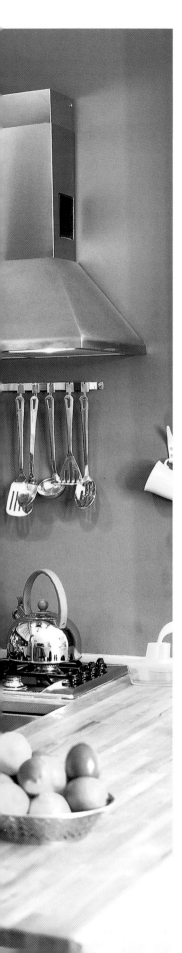

# Small but streamlined

## Keep the mix of materials and colours to a minimum to maximize the feeling of space in a compact kitchen.

Beech worktops and units teamed with metallic-finish appliances and a dramatic wall colour give a kitchen with real impact.

In a small kitchen you need to decide where your priorities lie. Here, a base cupboard has been sacrificed to fit in a dishwasher, which in turn means only a small round sink is necessary, freeing up more of the worksurface. The wall of cupboards is broken up with central panels of frosted glass with a square detail and handles in sweeping arcs of polished chrome, adding the touches of interest you need if you choose the same material for both worktop and cupboards.

Deep purple is an unusual choice for a kitchen but looks fabulous with both the metal and wood. The only other colour in the kitchen comes from small details like wall-hung mugs and a bowl of fruit.

### What else would work?

- deep red walls
- open shelving
- granite worktop

▲ Most appliances are now available in a metallic finish. In this kitchen, everything from the fridge to the dishwasher, cooker, toaster and microwave come in the same finish.

▲ Look out for storage solutions. This hanging rack provides a draining system above the sink to free up worktop space.

▲ Make full use of high ceilings with tall units; you could also fit downlighters into the overhanging top to illuminate the worksurface.

# Colourful kitchens

Who said kitchens should be white or wood? Make colour the defining feature of your kitchen and create a room with real personality. Use the walls, floor and units to form dramatic blocks of colour. Choose a different shade for each one and keep all the other elements in the kitchen white or steel to avoid turning a bold scheme into a discordant jumble of colours.

Go for a colourful kitchen if you enjoy setting your own mark on your home. A colourful kitchen is the chance to be a bit quirky and have fun with a theme, perhaps giving the room retro touches, or repeating bright motifs. This is a relaxed look that can bring warmth and life, particularly to small kitchens.

# Painted fridge

Appliances have been white for so long that we sometimes forget they don't need to be. Turn an old fridge into a feature with a coat of spray paint.

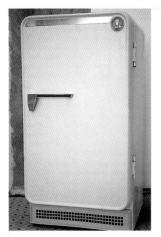

⧗ **2 HOURS**

**You will need**
- fine-grade sandpaper
- soft cloth
- white spirit
- newspaper or polythene sheeting
- masking tape
- enamel spray paint primer
- enamel spray paint
- protective masks

**1** Move to a well-ventilated area. Using fine-grade sandpaper, lightly remove any rust patches and sand the surface until smooth. Wash down, then clean again with a cloth wrung out in white spirit.

**2** Protect the surrounding area with plenty of newspaper or polythene sheeting. Mask off any areas of fridge you do not want to paint (such as the rubber seal around the door, the handle and trim).

**3** Prime the fridge, holding can 30–40cm (12–16in) away from the surface, and move it slowly from right to left. If the paint runs, you are spraying too close or too heavily. Leave to dry.

**4** Apply the spray paint in the same way, applying as many coats of paint as needed to get smooth coverage.

# Mexican border

Give plain units a fresh new look by painting them and adding your own colourful hand-made border.

**1** Clean the doors thoroughly, sand lightly and wipe down with a cloth wrung out in white spirit.

**2** Apply the yellow base colour to the doors. Dilute the blue paints one part water to one part paint and paint one sheet of paper in light blue and one sheet in dark blue. Leave to dry.

**2 HOURS** plus drying

### You will need
- sandpaper
- cloth
- white spirit
- yellow, dark blue and light blue emulsion paint
- paintbrushes
- large sheets of thin white paper
- PVA glue
- sponge
- acrylic varnish

**3** Tear the dark blue sheet into strips around 3cm (1⅛in) wide. Tear carefully, but allow the edges to be slightly uneven for interest. Tear the pale blue sheets into strips around 1cm (⅜in) wide and then cut out leaf shapes.

**4** Thin a little PVA glue with water until it is runny. Paste the back of a dark blue strip thoroughly and smooth on to the door with a damp sponge. Apply pale blue strips either side in the same way. When dry, decorate the dark blue strip with the leaf shapes.

**5** When dry, varnish the whole door with a few coats of acrylic varnish.

# Open shelving

Adapt a wall unit to give you extra storage by fitting shelves to hold kitchen equipment.

⧗ 1½ **HOURS** plus drying

**You will need**
- screwdriver
- tape measure
- 12mm (½in) MDF
- saw
- primer
- vinyl silk paint in two colours
- paintbrush
- pencil
- drill
- screws

**1** Lay the wall unit on its back on the floor. Remove the doors. Carefully measure the interior width and depth of the cupboard and cut your extra shelves from MDF.

**2** Prime and paint the outside and inside of the cupboard in one colour, and the inside back of the cupboard in a contrasting colour. Prime and paint the shelves in the same colour as the inside back of the cupboard, but paint the edges to match the unit exterior. Leave to dry.

**3** With the unit lying on its back, hold the first shelf in position. Use a pencil to mark its position inside the cupboard, then measure and mark where the screw holes will go on the outside of the cupboard. Remove the shelf and drill the holes, then replace the shelf in position and screw firmly in place. Repeat for all the shelves. Touch up the paint finish where required.

# Metallic squares

Spray paint squares onto these bland cupboard doors to create a lively, colourful look.

**1** It is easier if you remove the doors first and work in a well-ventilated area. If you cannot remove the doors, follow the instructions below but make sure the areas surrounding each door are well protected and that the windows are open. Lay the door flat on a large area of newspaper and mark out squares using a pencil and steel rule – use the set square to check squares are exact.

**2** Mask off both squares on each door, using masking tape and newspaper to ensure all the areas of the door you do not wish to spray are well covered.

**3** Shake the can of paint well and start to spray, using a steady side-to-side motion. Aim to build up several layers of light coats, keeping motion side-to-side, for an even finish. Leave to dry completely before removing the masking tape and rehanging the doors.

**45** MINUTES
**per door**

### You will need
- screwdriver
- masking tape
- pencil
- steel rule
- set square
- metallic spray paint, suitable for your kitchen unit door surface
- newspaper

# Technicolor tiles

Revamp your worktop by laying a colourful new tiled top. You'll be amazed at how dramatically it changes the whole look of the room.

 **1 DAY**

## You will need
- 4cm (1½in) battens
- saw
- primer
- oil-based paint
- tacks
- hammer
- tape measure
- pencil
- tile adhesive
- notched spreader
- tiles
- tile spacers
- tile cutter
- tile nibblers
- sponge
- waterproof grout
- soft cloth

**1** Cut battens to length to form the edge of the worktop. Prime, then paint them to match your kitchen. Tack on to the front edge of the worktop so that the top protrudes a tile's thickness above the existing worksurface.

**2** Work out your design by measuring the worktop. The first row of tiles will go along the front edge. If you will end up having to cut tiles to fit the edges, find the centre of the worktop and work out from that point.

**3** Spread adhesive over about 60cm (2ft) square at a time. Press the tiles in position, using tile spacers to ensure that the gaps for grouting are even. Cut tiles to fit the edges using a tile cutter and nibblers. Remove excess adhesive with a damp sponge and leave to dry.

**4** Apply the grout, removing excess with a sponge, then polish the tiles with a dry, soft cloth.

# Essential memo board

This takes little more than blackboard paint and a sheet of MDF, but it will prove to be the most indispensable item in your kitchen.

⏳ **1½ HOURS**
plus drying

**You will need**
• 12mm (½in) MDF cut to size
• primer
• paintbrush
• blackboard paint
• 4 metal corners
• pencil
• drill
• screws
• screwdriver
• spirit level
• tape measure
• 2 sturdy hooks
• wallplugs

**1** Prime the front and back of the sheet of MDF and leave to dry. Apply two even coats of blackboard paint to the front and sides of the MDF, leaving to dry thoroughly between each coat.

**2** Position the metal corners in place and use a pencil to mark the positions of the screw holes. Drill holes through the MDF at the pencil marks, then screw the corners securely in place.

**3** Mark the positions of the wall hooks, checking with a spirit level that they will hold the blackboard straight. Hold each hook in turn up to the wall and mark the screw hole positions. Drill holes, insert wallplugs and screw the hooks to wall. Rest the board on the hooks.

# Squares of brightness

## Colourful batik

● If your tablecloth is new, wash, dry and iron it first. Follow the instructions on your batik kit to paint on your chosen design. This tablecloth has been decorated with ever-decreasing squares.
Put the cloth in to the washing machine with dye, according to the manufacturer's instructions.

**2 HOURS**

**You will need**
• white or pale tablecloth
• batik kit
• fabric dye
• paintbrush

## Picture wall

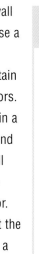

● Measure the area of wall you want to cover and use a pencil to mark out a rectangle which will contain all the pictures and mirrors. Position the first mirror in a corner of the rectangle and mark where the hook will go. Hammer in a picture hook and hang the mirror. Repeat for the mirrors at the other three corners. Use a tape measure to find the mid-point between the mirrors and hang one mirror centrally in each of the top and bottom rows. Hold the middle-row mirrors in place to find where the hooks should go and hang them in place, too. Put the greetings cards in clip frames and hang the pictures centrally between the mirrors.

**30 MINUTES**

**You will need**
• tape measure
• pencil
• spirit level
• 8 square mirrors (preferably distorting mirrors)
• 7 greetings cards
• 7 clip frames
• 15 picture hooks
• 15 masonry nails
• hammer
• picture wire

## Mosaic splashback

• Mark out the area that you want as your splashback. Make sure the wall is clean and dry and fill any cracks or gaps. Apply tile adhesive to a small area at a time and press individual tiles into the adhesive to create a random pattern. Continue spreading and fixing tiles until the whole wall is covered. Leave to set and then grout, wiping away excess with a cloth.

⏳ **45** MINUTES

**You will need**
• pencil and ruler
• selection of mosaic tiles
• all-in-one tile adhesive and grout
• notched adhesive spreader
• cloth

# Fun felt squares

• Cut the felt to the same size as the tile, plus an allowance of 5cm (2in) all round. Peel off the tile backing and stretch the felt over the adhesive side of the cork tile. Fold over the excess felt neatly and stick down at the back using strong sticky tape. Glue or screw to a wall and use as a pinboard.

⏳ **15** MINUTES

**You will need**
• felt
• self-adhesive cork tile
• scissors
• strong sticky tape

# Clever touches

## Sunshine blind

• Lay the blind on the cutting mat. Mark out your design on a piece of thin card. This project has used a 7 cm square, divided into four smaller squares. Cut out the design from the card and work out how it will repeat across the blind. Lightly pencil in horizontal guides across the blind to help you line up the template. Tape the template in place and draw around the inside of each cut out square to move the design on to the blind. Repeat until the design is drawn right across the blind in two rows. Carefully cut out squares using a craft knife.

A useful tip is to make sure your design does not leave flimsy strips of material between the cut out shapes or the blind will sag.

⏳ **1½ HOURS** 🖌

**You will need**
• roller blind
• cutting mat
• pencil
• craft knife
• ruler
• sticky tape
• eraser

## Can herb planters

• Wash the cans well and pierce a few drainage holes in the bottom of each. Add a handful of gravel, then fill the cans with compost to 1cm (⅜in) below the rim. Scatter the herb seeds evenly and sprinkle with another thin layer of compost. Water and keep in a sunny position.

⏳ **10 MINUTES** 🖌

**You will need**
• cans with decorative labels
• awl
• fine gravel
• potting compost
• herb seeds

## Fridge magnets

- Select colourful photos or postcards with a food theme. Stick each on to a piece of thin card cut to the same size. Attach flexible self-adhesive magnets to the back and stick on the fridge door.

**15 MINUTES**

### You will need
- selection of postcards or photos
- glue
- thin card
- craft knife and ruler
- cutting mat
- flexible self-adhesive magnets

## Recipe splashback

- Choose favourite recipes torn from magazines, written out on paper or photocopied from books. Place a piece of masking tape in each corner of the Perspex sheet and drill screw holes. Drill holes in the wall to match and insert wallplugs. Arrange the recipes as you would like them and use spray adhesive to fix them to the underside of the Perspex sheet. Screw the splashback in place.

**1 HOUR**

### You will need
- selection of recipes on paper
- masking tape
- 5mm (¼in) sheet of Perspex, cut to size by glazier
- drill
- wallplugs
- spray adhesive
- dome-headed screws

# Dress it up

## Concealing curtain

• Cut the fabric to twice the width of the opening, adding 5cm (2in) all round for hems. Sew hems on all four sides, leaving the edges open at the top of the curtain to insert cord. If there is no convenient place to fix cup hooks into either side of the opening, cut pieces of batten and fix either side. Screw cup hooks into the sides of the opening, thread cord through the top of the curtain and hook over the cup hooks.

⏳ **30** MINUTES

**You will need**
• fabric or old tablecloth
• sewing machine or needle and thread
• strong elasticated cord with hooks or eyes at each end
• cup hooks
• wood batten (if required)

## Retro style

• Paint the door in a base colour and leave to dry. Cut out the images and plan their positioning on the door. Apply wallpaper paste to the backs of the images and fix them in place on the door, using a soft, clean cloth to smooth out any air bubbles and wipe away excess paste. Leave to dry thoroughly, then apply several coats of clear matt varnish.

⏳ **1½** HOURS

**You will need**
• water-based paint
• paintbrush
• colour photocopies of images (postcards, magazine pictures etc)
• sharp scissors
• wallpaper paste and brush
• soft cloth
• clear matt polyurethane varnish

## Colourful blackboard door

• Mark a 5cm (2in) border around the edges of the door and mask off the inside. Paint around the border with oil-based paint. Leave to dry, then remove the masking tape. Now mask off the painted border and paint inside with blackboard paint using even strokes. Leave to dry thoroughly before carefully removing the masking tape.

## Instant sheer curtain

• Fix the curtain pole in place above the window. Measure the height of the window and cut the fabric to twice the height, plus 10cm (4in). Hem the raw edges and iron. Drape the fabric over the pole and gather it up at the front to knot loosely in place.

# Zest for life

Cheer up your kitchen with bright citrus colours and bring a hint of Mediterranean sunshine to even the cloudiest of days. Combining shades of lime, lemon and orange gives added vitality and a feeling of extra warmth.

▲ Why stick with boring white when your microwave, kettle, toaster and other small appliances can be part of your colour scheme?

▼ Colour-coordinated cutlery, tablecloth, napkins and placemats will give every mealtime a sunny feel.

▲ Use a craft knife to cut placemats from sheets of flexible plastic and carve out names or words to suit your guests, or the occasion.

▲   Coordinated tableware in a multitude of citrus colours makes every meal look special. Pick out individual shades for napkins, cloths and cutlery.

▲   Hollow out a lemon, melt a candle in a pan, then fill the lemon with the hot wax. Leave until it starts to set before inserting a wick.

▲   Bright yellow chairs and cheerful gerberas are all it has taken to make this small breakfast area a sun-filled corner of the room.

Colourful kitchens

# The colours of the rainbow

There are many different, instant ways of bringing colour into the kitchen without having to repaint the walls or change all the cupboards or units. Below are a few ideas to add a little zest to your kitchen.

▲ Even everyday objects can be fun if you choose beautiful sorbet shades for bowls and food savers.

▼ Sturdy canvas shopping bags have a multitude of uses in the kitchen. Use them to hold newspapers for recycling, vegetables, bottles – even your shopping!

▲ Instead of pastels or bright colours, colour-theme your tableware in spicy earth hues.

▲ Wrap individual sets of knives and forks in pretty coloured napkins and pile all the wrapped sets into a basket for a fun and informal way to dress the table.

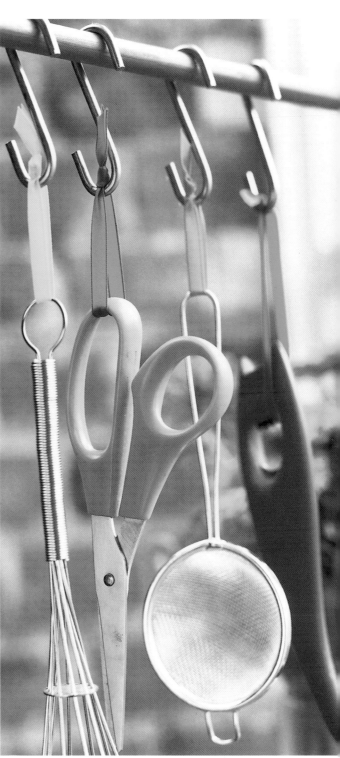

▲ Look for bins, bowls and bags to liven up every part of the kitchen. Choose a variety of colours but keep to the same tone and they will always look good together.

▲ Make a hanging rail by painting a length of dowelling, adding butcher's hooks and hang up utensils on loops of coloured ribbon.

Colourful kitchens

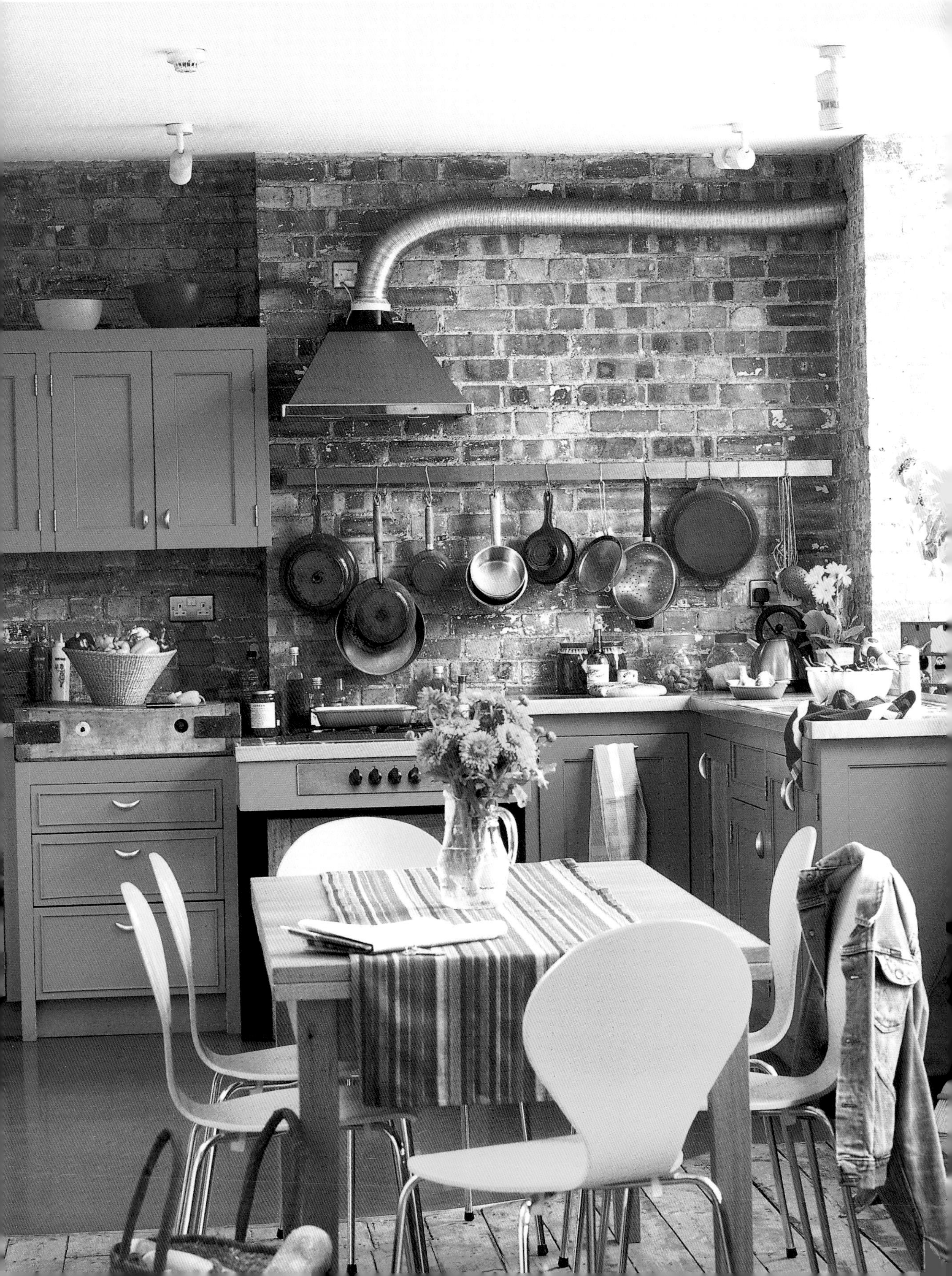

# Colour it bright

## Sea-green cupboards contrast with rich reds and sunny yellows.

Bare brick walls are the starting point for this kitchen, inspiring the brick red floor and deep orange-red pans. The wonderful blue-green colour complements the warmth of the reds perfectly, while hints of yellow in the chairs, flowers and details like the tea towel are the injection of surprising colour that brings the room alive and gives it maximum impact.

Wooden worktops are a natural choice with the rough brick walls and the bare floorboards in the eating area. Although stripped pine floors look great, they are not practical for the cooking area unless well sealed. Use vinyl, linoleum or rubber flooring instead for the area most vulnerable to water and grease spills.

Touches like the green plastic broom and cheerful striped tablecloth give this kitchen a retro hint. Everything else is kept simple with stainless steel and chrome.

### What else would work?

- beech chairs
- whitewashed walls
- bold yellow units
- beech venetian blind

▲ Even fruit and vegetables can become part of your kitchen's look. Bowls of sweet peppers or lemons are great for adding colour.

▲ A fun and informal multi-coloured tablecloth adds to the lively look of the kitchen.

▲ A pan rail not only frees up cupboard space but lets you make a show of colourful enamel pans.

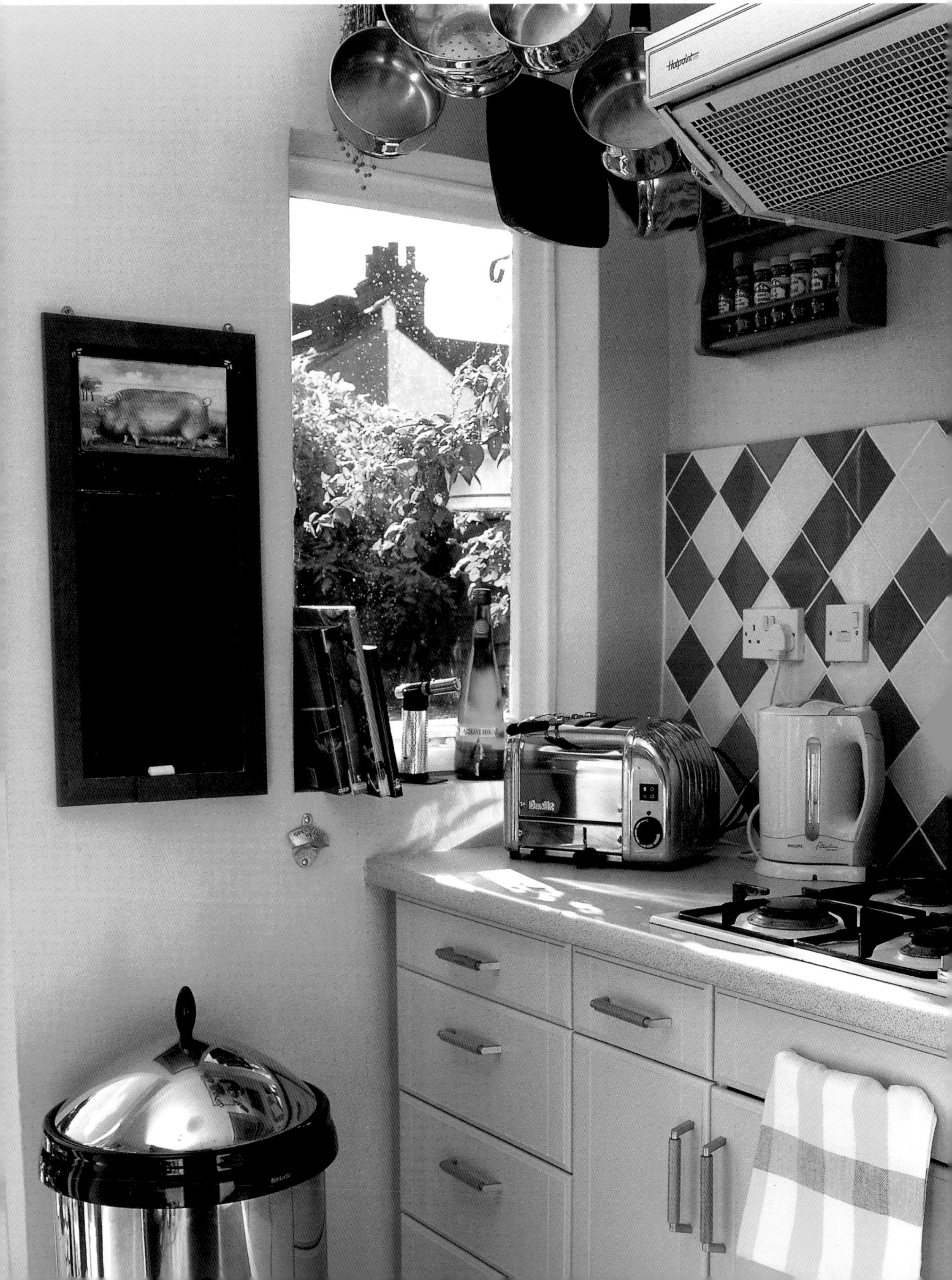
Hotpoint
AQUALIBRA
Dualit
PHILIPS

# Buttercup and mint

## The sunny yellow walls are the key to a kitchen that can't fail to lift your spirits.

Kitchen units in a subtle pastel shade can become the base for many different looks. Here they are set against a bright, rich yellow on the walls that fills the kitchen with sunshine. The crimson, yellow and green tiles make a real feature of the splashback. Laying tiles on the diagonal like this, rather than in rows, gives the illusion of more space in a limited area. With such strong colours, choose worktops, flooring and appliances that will fade into the background and not fight for attention.

In a small kitchen, look for ways to create more storage space, like the spice rack and utensil rail on the wall and the hanging rack over the worktop. The blackboard, spice rack and toaster add an old-fashioned flavour which makes this kitchen seem even more welcoming.

### What else would work?

- tiles in shades of aqua, turquoise and blue
- granite worktop
- stainless steel appliances
- cream units

▲ Make the most of every space in a small kitchen with a hanging rack. The ideal kind are those that can be raised and lowered on a rope pulley, like an old-fashioned drying rack.

▲ If you don't need curtains or blinds for privacy, leave the window undressed and let in the light.

▲ Changing cupboard handles can transform the style of the whole room.

▲ Painted units give you the ultimate in versatile kitchens. When you fancy a new look, simply repaint them in a different colour. It should guarantee that you never grow bored with your kitchen.

▲ Keep accessories in the same strict colour palette or you will lose the impact.

▲ In a small kitchen, try to build in appliances. Freestanding ones break up the line of units and make the room look fragmented and smaller.

# A kitchen with real impact

## No view and short on space? Defy convention with colour you can't ignore.

It's tempting to go for light, bright colours in a small space, but this kitchen shows how effective it can be to turn conventional wisdom on its head and fill the space with rich, deep colour instead. It works because the colours have been used in bold swathes over the units and on the walls.

The same deep indigo for the floor and the cupboards creates a well of colour in the lower half of the kitchen and the white splashback provides a visual break and throws the raspberry red into contrast. Limited touches of yellow around the room draw your eye from the sink to the corner to the top of the units, making the room feel larger, and metallic sink, cooker and pots bring sparkle to the room.

### What else would work?

• white floor
• touches of lime green
• silver-tiled splashback
• white laminate worktop

# Shaker style

With Shaker there's no distinction between style and function – every detail has a purpose. We have adapted the look to suit modern living, but the Shaker kitchen is still essentially simple and functional.

The key style elements of a Shaker kitchen are painted units with framed panel doors, turned wooden door knobs, wooden worktops and practical tiled floors. Pots, pans, tables and chairs should all be pared down in design, with no fussy details. The Shakers invented ingenious storage solutions, such hanging kitchen chairs out of the way on peg rails. You can use almost any colour in a Shaker kitchen but for the most authentic look, choose pale greens and blues, terracotta, ochre and cream. Mix and match your favourite aspects of Shaker style with the comfort and convenience of modern appliances and materials to create a kitchen that combines the best of all worlds.

# Woodgrained peg rail

A peg rail is probably the single most recognizable Shaker design element. It has so many uses from storage to simple, yet effective, display ideas and fits in almost anywhere. Make it look authentic with this woodgrain effect.

⏳ **I HOUR**
plus drying

**You will need**
- peg rail
- cream emulsion
- slate blue emulsion
- scumble glaze
- woodgraining tool

**1** Paint the rail with a cream base coat and leave to dry.

**2** Mix scumble glaze into the slate blue emulsion, one part scumble glaze to three parts emulsion. Paint over the base coat.

**3** While the top coat is still wet, draw the toothed graining tool across the surface, rocking it gently back and forth to create a woodgrain effect. Leave to dry.

# Folk art chairs

An ordinary kitchen chair can be turned into something special with a simple sponged design.

**▮ DAY**

**You will need**
- woodwash in yellow, rust and blue
- large and small paintbrushes
- tape measure
- pencil
- dense foam
- ruler
- craft knife
- cutting mat
- saucers for woodwash

**1** Paint the chairs with the yellow woodwash and leave to dry. Measure your chair back and divide by four to give you the size of the diamonds. Cut out a diamond from the foam using a craft knife. Dip foam into the rust woodwash and press the stamp on to the chair. Repeat to form a line of diamonds.

**2** Now cut the diamond-shaped foam in half to make a trianglular shape. Dip it in the woodwash and decorate the edges of the chair with triangles.

**3** Pour some blue woodwash into a saucer and use a small paintbrush to paint dots in the spaces between the diamonds and on the triangles on the edges of the chair.

# Tongue and groove panelling

Shaker rooms were often panelled, and adding tongue and groove panelling to some or all of your kitchen walls gives a practical and attractive finish. Take it to windowsill or dado height.

⏳ **| DAY**

### You will need
- 25mm (1in) softwood battens
- tape measure
- pencil
- spirit level
- drill
- wallplugs
- 5cm (2in) screws
- screwdriver
- tongue and groove boards
- saw
- hammer
- 25cm (1in) panel pins
- nail punch
- woodfiller
- sandpaper
- moulding or peg rail

**1** Attach the battens horizontally on the wall. Mark out their positions 40cm (16in) apart, checking with a spirit level that they are horizontal. Drill holes through the battens at about 30cm (1ft) intervals, hold up to the wall and mark the positions of the drill holes. Drill wall holes as marked, and insert wallplugs. Screw the battens to the wall.

**2** Measure and mark out where the boards will go and cut to size. Position the first board against the wall with the groove on the left side. Check it is perfectly upright.

**3** Nail the panel to the battens using panel pins.

**4** Slide the next board on and gently tap in place with a hammer, using an offcut of wood to protect the board's edge. Nail in place. Repeat to cover the wall.

**5** Punch in the pin heads below the surface of the wood. Fill in the pin holes with woodfiller and sand smooth. Finish with a moulding or peg rail along the top.

# Shaker-style doors

A plain frame added to flat-fronted cupboard doors is a simple way of giving them greater character while keeping the simple Shaker style.

**1** Remove the doors from the cupboards, lay flat and sand all over to provide a key. Measure the height of the doors and cut two lengths of MDF to this length for the upright parts of the frame. Glue and pin in place, then leave to dry.

**2** Measure the width of the door between the upright parts of the frame and cut two pieces of MDF to this length. Glue and pin in place, then leave to dry.

**3** Punch in the pin heads below the surface of the wood and use woodfiller to disguise them. Sand to a smooth finish. Paint the whole door with eggshell paint and leave to dry before fixing on the pewter door knobs.

⧖ **3** HOURS

### You will need
- sandpaper
- tape measure
- pencil
- 8mm (⁵⁄₁₆in) MDF, 5cm (2in) wide
- tenon saw
- strong wood glue
- panel pins
- nail punch
- woodfiller
- eggshell paint
- pewter door knobs

# Fresh blue and white

## Laundry basket liner

 Fold the fabric in half, top to bottom, and stitch up the sides to within 5cm (2in) of the top. Fold the top back on itself and stitch all round the top of the bag to make a channel for the cord. Leave one side unstitched so that you have an opening through which to insert the cord. Turn the bag right side out and thread the cord through the stitched channel, knotting the cords at the end. Place the liner in the laundry basket.

 **I HOUR**

**You will need**
- sheeting or cotton fabric
- sewing machine or needle and thread
- white cord
- scissors

## Breakfast checks

 Sand the eggcup to remove any varnish. Paint with white emulsion and leave to dry. Paint on horizontal stripes with blue emulsion paint and leave to dry before painting on vertical stripes. Finish with a coat of varnish.

**30 MINUTES** plus drying

**You will need**
- wooden eggcup
- sandpaper
- paintbrush
- white emulsion
- blue emulsion
- matt acrylic varnish

## Glass cloth café curtains

- Check the length of the cloths against the window and mark the height. Stretch the net rod out to the full width of the window at this height and fix in place. Attach curtain clips at 3–4cm (1½in) intervals to the rod and simply clip on the cloths.

**⧗ 10 MINUTES**

**You will need**
- 2 glass cloths or tea towels
- pencil
- net rod
- curtain clips
- tape measure

## Tea towel cushion cover

- Wash and dry the cloth before you start. Iron smooth, then lay the cloth right side up and fold one short end to the middle of the cloth. Fold the opposite end up to overlap the first by 2cm (1in). Pin together and stitch up the sides. Remove the pins, turn right side out and press. Stitch press studs across the opening at regular distances, then stitch buttons over the top to decorate. Insert the cushion pad through the opening.

**⧗ 30 MINUTES**

**You will need**
- tea towel or glass cloth
- pins
- sewing machine
- needle and thread
- 3 press studs
- 3 mother of pearl buttons
- 30 x 40cm (12 x 16in) cushion pad

# Shaker motifs

## Studded heart

• Remove the cupboard door and lay it on a flat surface. Lay the paper template on the wire mesh and, wearing gloves, cut out a heart shape, smoothing down any sharp edges as you go. Position the heart on the door and

⏳ **I HOUR** 🖊

**You will need**
• paper template of heart shape
• fine-gauge wire mesh
• thick gloves
• wire cutters
• tacks
• hammer

hammer in tacks at the bottom point and at the top to hold in position. Hammer in tacks all the way around the heart, evenly spaced. Decorate the edge of the door with more tacks and rehang.

## Sweet lavender bag

• Cut a heart-shaped paper template. Fold a fabric remnant in half, pin the template to the fabric and cut out, to give you two fabric hearts. Pin the right sides together, and sew around the edge, leaving a 4cm (1½in) opening. Turn

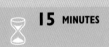

⏳ **I5 MINUTES** 🖊

**You will need**
• paper
• scissors
• fabric remnants
• pins
• needle and thread
• dried lavender
• twine

right side out, attach small squares of contrasting fabric for decoration, then fill with lavender. Slipstitch the opening closed. Sew on twine to hang up the bag.

## Kitchen table trim

• Measure the sides of the table and cut the pelmet to size. Prime the pelmet and undercoat the table. When completely dry, tack the pelmet lengths in place along the edges of the table. Punch in the tack heads below the surface and fill with woodfiller. Give the newly fashioned table two top coats of oil-based paint, leaving the paint to dry between coats.

**2 HOURS**
**plus drying**

**You will need**
• table
• tape measure
• pencil
• shaped MDF pelmet
• saw
• MDF primer
• white undercoat
• paintbrush
• tacks
• hammer
• nail punch
• woodfiller
• white oil-based paint

## Gingham tile transfers

• Clean tiles thoroughly with white spirit and a soft cloth. Aim to create a border pattern three tiles wide so that you can add an inset pattern into the middle row of the tiles here and there.

**20 MINUTES**

**You will need**
• white spirit
• soft cloth
• tile transfers

Peel off the tile transfer facing, smooth on to the tile and peel off the backing. Repeat all the way along the splashback.

# Shaker motifs

Checks and hearts were popular Shaker motifs and would appear in everything from fabric and metalware to wood carvings and woven baskets.

▲ A simple wooden peg rail is a good place to hang everyday necessities like small brushes, tea towels and peg bags. Attach loops of gingham ribbon to pretty up ordinary objects.

▲ Make a neat Roman blind using a kit from a department store. Crisp checks bring the right note of homely simplicity.

▼ Get that kitchen roll off the worktop with a wall-mounted iron holder with a heart motif. If you can't find something similar, you can easily make one using a wire coat hanger bent into shape and sprayed with black paint.

▲ A hand-woven basket in your kitchen colours is a charming way to store table linens and tea towels. It gives you more cupboard space and makes your linens easily accessible, too.

▲ Aluminium canisters are ideal for storing washing powders, liquids and soaps. They look smarter than a collection of packets and keep everything dry. Use alphabet stencils and ceramic paint dabbed on with a stencil brush to create labels for them.

▲ Wind strips of fabric around the handles and edges of wicker or cane baskets and use them for anything from holding clothes pegs to bread or cutlery.

▲ Use colours that softly complement one another to paint cupboards with different uses. Here the storage units are a muted green while the big pan and utensil drawers of the central island are off-white.

# Making the details count

Shakers were especially noted for their neat storage solutions and numerous small, practical ideas to make the home run more efficiently, from plant pots to laundry baskets.

▼ Authentic Shaker birch boxes can be quite expensive to buy. Bring the look to your kitchen by choosing a small, affordable one to use as a pot holder for country garden flowers.

▲ Make a real feature of spring bulbs by potting up each one in its own enamel mug. Set the bulb so that it sits halfway out of the potting compost and dress the top with moss. Keep the soil just damp by watering sparingly.

▲ If you are having a wooden worktop fitted in your kitchen, get the fitter to leave you with the offcuts. Endgrain worktops particularly make great chopping boards. Like the worktop, make sure you oil it regularly to keep it in good condition.

▲ Cereals left in open packets quickly go soft and stale. Decant them into good glass jars with airtight stoppers. They'll look attractive enough to on display.

▲ Make laundry days easier by separating out your washing as it mounts. Use a different basket for coloureds, whites and delicates so that they are ready to carry straight to the washing machine and back again.

# A garden theme

Create an irresistibly pretty kitchen with classic cream units and bright sprigged fabric with a theme of fruit, flowers and vegetables.

Painted cream units were the starting point for this light, bright kitchen, and a fresh flower and vegetable print inspired the idea of bringing the outside indoors. The theme is continued in the coordinating border around the top of the room, the hops and fresh flowers and the miniature bird boxes.

Tongue and groove panelling, varnished to protect it against spills and stains, is a great solution for kitchen walls and has a suitably hand-crafted feel. Use white emulsion diluted with water as a woodwash, then coat with clear, satin-finish varnish.

Modern appliances can be difficult to integrate into this type of kitchen, but here the washing machine has been neatly hidden behind a curtain.

## What else would work?

- kitchen units in pale green
- terracotta floor tiles
- gingham fabrics
- Roman blind at the window

▲ Hunt around junk shops for an old table and chairs like these which can be rubbed down and painted to match your kitchen.

▲ Bringing in touches of the garden adds enormously to the style. Hop bines are inexpensive and last well.

▲ Items with functional simplicity, such as this wooden drainer, hit the right note.

# Shaker goes modern

## Blend pared-down Shaker style with modern assets.

It's easy to update the Shaker look because its simplicity makes it a natural partner for clean, modern lines. Despite being obviously modern in style, this room still owes its roots to the Shaker tradition, with framed doors and wood worktops. The hi-tech stainless steel cooker and hood make a dramatic focal point and contemporary metal handles replace the traditional round wooden knobs. The white floor tiles make the room feel clean and bright, while laying them 'brick style', in staggered rows, gives a less formal effect.

If you have room, even a small island is an invaluable addition to the kitchen. Make sure the worktop on it is a minimum of 15cm (6in) wider than the base unit and you can use it as a breakfast bar as well as a handy preparation surface. Cupboards underneath, extra big pots and the hanging rack above maximize storage – an important factor in Shaker homes.

### What else would work?

- stone-coloured walls
- beech laminate flooring
- duck-egg blue units
- round wooden handles

▲ A glass cabinet panel, frosted in stripes, echoes the grooved door panels in the rest of the kitchen.

▲ Traditional Shaker boxes are beautifully crafted and provide useful storage to hide away those little bits and pieces that accumulate so quickly.

▲ The kitchen stool is definitely a twenty-first-century addition, yet it fits in well with the style of the rest of the room.

▲ The ragged edges to the terracotta floor tiles have been made by tumbling them, giving them an aged appearance that suits this kitchen better than sharp squares.

▲ Wicker fits in well with the other natural materials used here, and these baskets provide roomy, airy storage for vegetables.

▲ No Shaker would recognize this lighting, but its highly functional design and unobtrusive styling fit well with Shaker principles.

# The natural touch

**Mix cream with earthy greens, browns and yellows for a calm, relaxing kitchen.**

Shaker kitchens work beautifully with natural materials and natural colours: cream panelled units, wooden worktops and a terracotta floor. The walls, in shades of cream, increase the sense of space, and the tiled splashback brings in beautifully toning shades of moss, lichen, cream and butter.

A central island houses a deep sink with a swan-necked tap and plenty of worksurface. The worktop for the other half of the kitchen is granite-look laminate which provides an interesting contrast. A freestanding butcher's block against the far wall is wonderfully practical, with a hanging rail for utensils, a shelf for spices, rack for knives, plus preparation space, which you can wheel to where you want it. There has been no attempt to hide away the kitchen appliances – some white, some stainless steel – yet nothing looks out of place in this relaxed and welcoming kitchen.

## What else would work?

- tiles in shades of blue
- cream dresser
- slate flooring
- pale green walls

# Index

# Acknowledgements

All pictures copyright of The National Magazine Company Limited, except for the following listed below:

**Marie-Louise Avery** 48 top left, 106 top right, 114 top left, 116 top left, 117 right, 117 top left, 117 bottom left
**B&Q PLC** 58–59, 59 top, 59 centre, 59 bottom
**Robert Bosch Domestic Appliances Ltd.** (tel;+44(0)1908 328 263)69 top left
**Crown Paints**/www.crownpaint.co.uk 46 top left
**Crown Wallcoverings & Home Furnishings** 70 bottom right
**Octopus Publishing Group Limited**/Shona Wood front cover bottom centre left, back cover centre right, 11
**Homelux** (stockists tel; +44(0)133 5340 340) 115 top left
**Parker Hobart**/www.divertimenti.co.uk(stockists tel; +44(0)7935 0689) 56–57, 57 top, 57 centre, 57 Bottom, 118 top left
**MFI** (stockists tel; +44(0)87069 5555)10 top right, 32–33, 33 top, 33 centre, 33 bottom, 122–123, 123 top, 123 centre, 123 bottom
**Quentin Hariott** 34 Top, 34 centre, 34 Bottom, 34–35
**Ronseal**/www.ronseal.co.uk (stockists tel; +44(0)114 240 9469) 46 bottom right
**The Symphony Group PLC**/www.symphony-group.co.uk (stockists tel; +44(0)800 555 876) 7
**Tony Timmington** 67
**Topps Tiles**/www.toppstiles.co.uk (stockists tel; +44(0)800 783 6262) 62 top right, 77 right

**Executive Editor:** Anna Southgate
**Editor:** Abi Rowsell
**Executive Art Editor:** Leigh Jones
**Designer:** Claire Harvey
**Picture Researcher:** Christine Junemann
*Your Home* **Picture Coordination:** Jill Morgan
**Production Controller:** Viv Cracknell